Free Downloads to Pep Up and Protect Your PC

Robert Penfold

Bernard Babani (publishing) Ltd
The Grampians
Shepherds Bush Road
London W6 7NF
England

www.babanibooks.com

Please note

Although every care has been taken with the production of this book to ensure that all information is correct at the time of writing and that any projects, designs, modifications, and/or programs, etc., contained herewith, operate in a correct and safe manner and also that any components specified are normally available in Great Britain, the Publisher and Author do not accept responsibility in any way for the failure (including fault in design) of any projects, design, modification, or program to work correctly or to cause damage to any equipment that it may be connected to or used in conjunction with, or in respect of any other damage or injury that may be caused, nor do the Publishers accept responsibility in any way for the failure to obtain specified components.

Notice is also given that if any equipment that is still under warranty is modified in any way or used or connected with home-built equipment then that warranty may be void.

© 2010 BERNARD BABANI (publishing) LTD

First Published - December 2010

British Library Cataloguing in Publication Data
A catalogue record for this book is available from the British Library

ISBN   978 0 85934 722 8

Cover Design by Gregor Arthur
Printed and bound in Great Britain for Bernard Babani (publishing) Ltd

Preface

Computer security is a subject that many computer users have ignored in the past, and they were probably taking little risk in doing so. Computer viruses made the news headlines from time to time, but the stories about impending worldwide doom never seemed to come to anything. Some viruses that were about to sweep the world actually turned up on less than a dozen computer systems. The degree of risk for the average computer user was very low, and the press tended to exaggerate the threat posed by the latest super-viruses.

Unfortunately, the computing world has radically changed in recent years and computer security is something that few can now afford to ignore. The speed with which some recent virus and worm attacks have spread around the world demonstrates how widespread use of the Internet has changed things. In the past it was mainly professionals looking after servers or large computer networks that had to worry about computer security, but it is now a subject that all computer users have to take seriously. Of course, the Internet has been around for many years, but it is now used by many more people and users tend to spend far longer online. Broadband Internet access opens up new possibilities, but it also makes computer systems far more vulnerable than ever before. The increasing use of Email as a quick and easy means of communicating with people all over the world has provided another means for viruses to spread. This threat has actually been the main cause for concern in recent times.

Fortunately, making a PC safe against hackers, viruses, and other nuisances does not require a high level of expertise, and does not have to cost very much. In fact there is plenty of good quality security software of various types that can be downloaded and kept up-to-date completely free This book explains in simple terms the differences between viruses, Trojans, and other harmful files, and how they can be combated using free software. It also covers the use of free firewalls to keep your PC free from the attentions of hackers.

In an ideal world you would set up a new PC to suit your requirements and then go on using it in trouble-free fashion for many years. Unfortunately, the realities of modern computing are rather different to the ideal. Most modern PCs tend to evolve over a period of time, with new software being installed, and probably new hardware and peripheral gadgets being added as well. The operating system has to change to accommodate this evolution, but each change has the potential for introducing problems. It seems to be quite normal for a computer to gradually slow down over a period of time unless steps are taken to keep the hard disc drives and operating system in optimum condition. This is again something that does not require a high degree of expertise, and it can be achieved at no cost using the built-in facilities of Windows and free software downloads. This book explains in simple terms the use of free tune-up suites, disc defragmenters, disc checkers, and other free software that will keep your computer running quickly and efficiently.

Robert Penfold

Trademarks

Microsoft, Windows, Windows XP, Windows Vista and Windows 7 are either registered trademarks or trademarks of Microsoft Corporation.

All other brand and product names used in this book are recognised trademarks, or registered trademarks of their respective companies. There is no intent to use any trademarks generically and readers should investigate ownership of a trademark before using it for any purpose.

Contents

1

Malware types 1

Safe downloading

There is plenty of good software available in the form of free downloads from the Internet, but there are also plenty of programs that are either completely bogus, or are the genuine article but with added malware of some kind. When downloading free software it is therefore important to only use reliable download sites where there is no significant risk of downloading infected software. It is also important to only download software that is well established and has a good reputation. New software that "promises the earth" might be a great new program, or it could be a "wolf in sheep's clothing".

In some cases it is possible to download free software from the software author's web site, or from the web site of the company that produces the software. Where possible, this represents the safest way of doing things. These days it seems to be quite normal for the web site of the software's originator to provide a link to one of the large download sites, rather than hosting the software themselves. Downloading software from one of these sites, such as CNET.com should be completely safe, because programs are checked for malware before they are accepted by the site.

Another important point to bear in mind is that most antimalware software and tuning programs should only be used with computers that are running under an appropriate operating system. This does not simply mean that you must use the Windows version of the program for a PC that is running under some form of Windows operating system. It will usually have to be a version of the program that is specifically intended for the particular version of Windows you are using. Always check that the recommended system requirements of the software match the equipment and exact operating system you are using. If there is a mismatch, do not try to download and install the software.

Malware types

From all sides

Computer security has been a growth industry in recent years, with ever more ways of protecting PCs being devised in response to increasingly imaginative ways of attacking them. Protecting your PC from various types of attack can be an expensive business. Apart from the initial outlay of buying the software, there is the on-going cost of keeping it up-to-date. This is not just a matter of ensuring that the software itself is the latest version. Of far greater importance, is the necessity of keeping the database of malware definitions up-to-date. The software stands little chance of detecting and dealing with any new malware unless it has the corresponding definitions in its database.

There is usually an annual fee for obtaining regular updates, and although the annual charge is not usually very high, the cost tends to build up over a few years. Eventually, the cost of protecting a computer from an Internet attack can exceed the initial purchase price of the computer! It is not essential to use a paid-for antivirus program and update service as there are completely free alternatives. Some of these alternatives are quite basic and do not provide anything approaching complete protection against computer malware. The best of these still have their uses, and they can be useful as a second line of defence. The better ones provide real-time protection in addition to the normal scanning capabilities, and they also have free updates available for the virus database.

Whether the best of the free antivirus programs provide the same degree of protection as the paid-for alternatives is a controversial subject. In the independent tests I have seen they usual do reasonably well against the commercial competition, and in my experience they have always performed well. Commercial antivirus software generally has more facilities, and the free programs are usually available in commercial versions that have more "bells and whistles". Whether the extra facilities are of real use to most users and actually provide a worthwhile increase in security is another matter. A good but free antivirus program should protect your PC from the common types of attack, and that is all that most home and small business users require. For larger business users the cost of comprehensive commercial security software is probably well justified.

Types of attack

Viruses are the best known form of computer attack, but there are other ways that hackers can mount an assault on your PC. In fact many of the much publicised computer viruses are not, strictly speaking, viruses at all. The non-technical press tend to call any form of software that attacks computers a virus. A virus is a specific type of program though, and represents just one of several types that can attack a computer. Initially, someone attaches the virus to a piece of software, and then finds a way of getting that software into computer systems. These days the Internet is the most likely route for the infection to be spread, but it is important not to overlook the fact that there are other means of propagating viruses. Indeed, computer viruses were being spread around the world long before the Internet came along.

Programs and possibly other files can carry viruses regardless of the source. If someone gives you a floppy disc, CD-ROM, or DVD containing software it is possible that the contents of the disc are infected with a virus. In the early days of personal computing the main route for viruses to spread was by way of discs containing illegally copied programs. Discs containing pirated software are still used to propagate viruses. Avoid any dodgy software if you wish to keep your PC virus-free.

Anyway, having introduced a virus into a system via one route or another, it will attack that system and try to replicate itself. Some viruses only attack the boot sector of a system disc. This is the part of the disc that the computer uses to boot into the operating system. Other viruses will try to attach themselves to any file of the appropriate type, which usually means a program file of some sort. The attraction of a program file is that the user will probably run the program before too long, which gives the virus a chance to spread the infection and (or) start attacking the computer system. At one time there were only two possible ways in which a virus could attack a computer. One way was for the virus to attach itself to a program file that the user then ran on his or her computer. The other was for someone to leave an infected floppy disc in the computer when it was switched off. On switching the computer on again the floppy disc was used as the boot disc, activating the virus in the disc's boot sector.

Script virus

These days you have to be suspicious of many more types of file. Many applications programs such as word processors and spreadsheets have the ability to automate tasks using scripts or macros as they are also known. The application effectively has a built-in programming language and the script or macro is a form of program. This makes it possible for viruses or other harmful programs to be present in many types of data file. Scripts are also used in some web pages, and viruses can be hidden in these JavaScript programs, Java applets, etc. There are other potential sources of infection such as Email attachments. I would not wish to give the impression that all files, web pages and Emails are potential sources of script or macro viruses. There are some types of file where there is no obvious way for them to carry a virus or other harmful program. A simple text file for example, should be completely harmless. Even in cases where a harmful program is disguised as a text file with a "txt" extension, the file should be harmless. The system will treat it as a text file and it can not be run provided no one alters the file extension. Similarly, an Email that contains a plain text message can not contain a script virus. Nevertheless, it is probably best to regard all files and Emails with a degree of suspicion. As explained later in this chapter, even though simple text can not carry a true virus, it can carry a virus of sorts.

Benign virus

It tends to be assumed that all viruses try to harm the infected computer system. This is not correct though, and many viruses actually do very little. For example, you might find that nothing more occurs than a daft message appears onscreen when a certain date is reached, or on a particular date each year. Viruses such as these certainly have a degree of nuisance value, but they are not harmful. I would not wish to give the impression that most viruses are harmless. Many computer viruses do indeed try to do serious damage to the infected system. If in doubt you have to assume that a virus is harmful.

Worm

A worm is a program that replicates itself, usually from one disc to another, or from one system to another via a local network or the Internet. Like a virus, a worm is not necessarily harmful. In recent times many of the worldwide virus scares have actually been caused by worms transmitted via Email, and not by what would normally be accepted as a virus. The usual ploy is for the worm to send a copy of itself to every address in the Email address book of the infected system. A worm spread in this way, even if it is not intrinsically harmful, can have serious consequences. There can be a sudden upsurge in the amount of Email traffic, possibly causing parts of the Email system to seriously slow down or even crash. Some worms compromise the security of the infected system, perhaps enabling it to be used by a hacker for sending spam for example.

Trojan horse

A Trojan horse, or just plain Trojan as it is now often called, is a program that is supposed to be one thing but is actually another. In the early days many Trojans were in the form of free software, and in particular free antivirus programs. The users obtained nasty shocks when the programs were run, with their computer systems being attacked. Like viruses, some Trojans do nothing more than display stupid messages, but others attack the disc files, damage the boot sector of the hard disc, and so on.

Backdoor Trojan

A backdoor Trojan is the same as the standard variety in that it is supplied in the form of a program that is supposed to be one thing but is actually another. In some cases nothing appears to happen when you install the program. In other cases the program might actually install and run as expected. In both cases one or two small programs will have been installed on the computer and set to run when the computer is booted.

One ploy is to have programs that produce log files showing which programs you have run and Internet sites that you have visited. The log will usually include any key presses as well. The idea is for the log file to provide passwords to things such as your Email account, online bank account, and so on. Someone hacking into your computer system will usually look for the log files, and could obviously gain access to important information from these files. Another ploy is to have a program that makes it easier for hackers to break into your computer system. A backdoor Trojan does not attack the infected computer in the same way as some viruses, and it does not try to spread the infection to other discs or computers. Potentially though, a backdoor Trojan is more serious than a virus, particularly if you use the computer for online banking, share dealing, etc. This is currently one of the most common types of computer malware.

Spyware

Spyware programs monitor system activity and send information to another computer by way of the Internet. There are really two types of spyware, and one of them tries to obtain passwords and send them to another computer. This takes things a step further than the backdoor Trojan programs mentioned earlier. A backdoor Trojan makes it easier for a hacker to obtain sensitive information from your PC, but it does not go as far as sending any information that is placed in the log files. Spyware is usually hidden in other software in Trojan fashion.

Adware

The second type of spyware is more correctly called adware. In common with spyware, it gathers information and sends it to another computer via the Internet. Adware is not designed to steal passwords or other security information from your PC. Its purpose is usually to gather information for marketing purposes, and this typically means gathering and sending details of the web sites you have visited. Some free programs are supported by banner advertising, and the adware is used to select advertisements that are likely to be of interest to you. Programs that are supported by adware have not always made this fact clear during the installation process. Sometimes the use of adware was pointed out in the End User License Agreement, but probably few people bother to read the "fine print". These days the more respectable software companies that use this method of raising advertising revenues make it clear that the adware will be installed together with the main program. There is often the option of buying a "clean" copy of the program. Others try to con you into installing the adware by using the normal tricks.

Dialers

A dialer is a program that uses a modem and an ordinary dial-up connection to connect your PC to another computer system. Dialers probably have numerous legitimate applications, but they are mainly associated with various types of scam. An early one was a promise of free pornographic material that required a special program to be downloaded. This program was, of course, the dialer which proceeded to call a high cost number in a country thousands of miles away. In due course the user received an astronomic telephone bill. A modern variation on this is where users are tricked into downloading a dialer, often with the promise of free software of some description. The user goes onto the Internet in the usual way via their dial-up connections, and everything might appear to be perfectly normal. What is actually happening though is that they are not connecting to the Internet via their normal Internet service provider (ISP). Instead, the dialler is connecting them to a different ISP that is probably thousands of miles away and is costing a fortune in telephone charges.   Again, the problem is very apparent when the telephone bill arrives.   The increasing use of broadband Internet connections has removed the threat of dialer related problems for many, but users of dial-up connections still need to guard against this problem.

Hoax virus

A hoax virus might sound innocuous enough and just a bit of a joke, but it has the potential to spread across the world causing damage to computer systems. The hoax is usually received in the form of an Email from someone that has contacted you previously. They say that the Email they sent you previously was infected with a virus, and the Email then goes on to provide information on how to remove the virus. This usually entails searching for one or more files on your PC's hard disc drive and erasing them. Of course, there was no virus in the initial Email. The person that sent the initial Email could be the hoaxer, or they might have been fooled by the hoax themselves. The hoax Email suggests that you contact everyone that you have emailed recently, telling them that their computer could be infected and giving them the instructions for the "cure". This is the main way in which a hoax virus is propagated. The files that you are instructed to remove could be of no real consequence, or they could be important system files. It is best not to fall for the hoax and find out which!

These hoax viruses demonstrate the point that all the antivirus software in the world will not provide full protection for your PC. They are simple text files that do not do any direct harm to your PC, and can not be kept at bay by software. Ultimately it is up to you to use some common sense and provide the final line of defence. A quick check on the Internet will usually provide details of hoax viruses and prevent you from doing anything silly.

Phishing

There are other scams that involve hoax emails, and there have been numerous instances of fake Emails being sent to customers of online financial companies. These purport to come from the company concerned, and they ask customers to provide their passwords and other account details. A link is provided to the site, and the site usually looks quite convincing. It is not the real thing though, and anyone falling for it has their account details stolen. These are called "phishing" attacks, and many millions of pounds have now been stolen in this way. The best defence against phishing attacks is to always go to financial sites via your normal route, such as typing the URL into the address bar or using an option in the favourites menu. Never use links provided in Emails.

Basic measures

The obvious way of protecting a PC from viruses and other harmful programs is to simply keep it away from possible sources of infection. Unfortunately, the quarantine approach is not usually a practical one. Little real world computing is compatible with this standalone approach. I use my PC to produce letters that are sent through the post, but I probably send about 100 times as many Emails, and receive about 100 Emails for every "snail mail" letter. I also receive data discs occasionally, and these have to be read using my computer. I have to use the Internet extensively for research, and I sometimes download software updates. Isolating my computer from the outside world would render it largely useless to me. Totally removing the threat of attack is not usually possible, but the chances of a successful attack can be greatly reduced by using a few basic precautions.

Email attachments

Some individuals operate a policy of never opening Email attachments. I do not take things that far, but I would certainly not open an Email attachment unless I knew the sender of the Email and was expecting the attachment. Bear in mind that some viruses and worms spread by hijacking a users Email address book and sending copies of the infected Email to every address in the address book. The fact that an Email comes from someone you know, or purports to, does not guarantee that it is free from infection. Another point to bear in mind is that Email attachments are now the most common way of spreading viruses and computer worms. Never activate a link in an Email unless you are sure that it is genuine and from a trustworthy source. The link might take your browser to a site that will attempt to attack your PC.

Selective downloading

Downloading software updates from the main computer software companies should be safe, as should downloading the popular freebies from their official sources. Downloading just about anything else involves a degree of risk and should be kept to a minimum. Never download and install any program unless you are sure that it is from a reliable source.

Pirate software

Pirated software has become a major problem for the software companies in recent years. In addition to casual software piracy where friends swap copies of programs there is now an epidemic of commercial copying. Apart from the fact that it is illegal to buy and use pirate software, unlike the real thing, some of it contains viruses, spyware, etc. A substantial percentage of the pirate software available for download on the Internet contains Trojans, viruses or other malware.

Built-in protection

Some programs, and particularly those from Microsoft, have built-in virus protection that is designed to block known macro/script viruses. If you have any programs that include this feature, make sure that it is enabled. Similarly, browsers often have one or more protection measures. Features such as these do not guarantee that your computer will be free from attacks and a certain amount of common sense has to be exercised, but it makes sense to use any built-in security measures that are available.

P2P

P2P (peer to peer) programs are widely used for file swapping. Even if you use this type of software for swapping legal (non-pirated) files, it still has to be regarded as very risky. In most cases you have no idea who is supplying the files, or whether they are what they are supposed to be. Also, you are providing others with access to your PC, and this access could be exploited by hackers.

Switch off

Some PC users leave their computers running continuously in the belief that it gives better reliability. It did in the days when computers were based on valves, but there is no evidence that it improves reliability with modern computers. It will increase your electricity bills, and it also increases the vulnerability of your PC if it has some form of always-on Internet connection. No one can hack into your computer system if it is switched off!

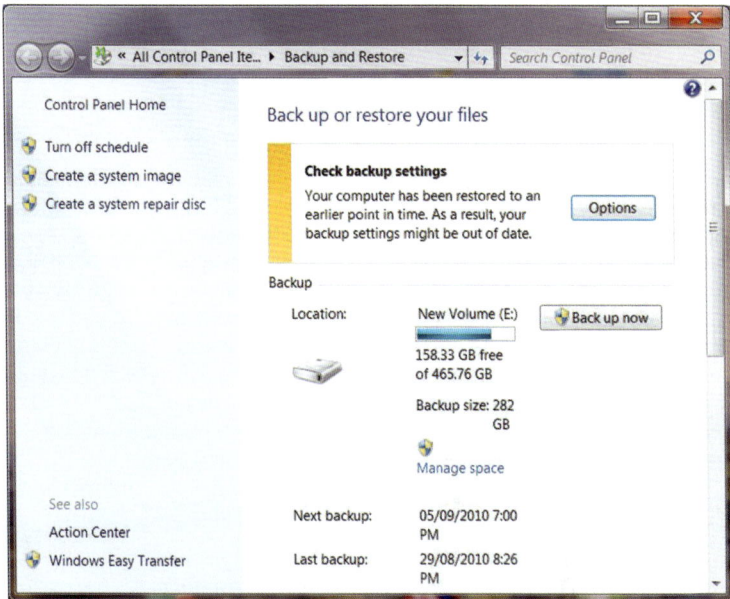

Fig.1.1 The Backup program of a modern version of Windows is a big improvement on earlier versions

Prevention

The old adage about "prevention is better than cure" certainly applies to computer viruses. In addition to some basic security precautions, equip your PC with antivirus software and keep it up-to-date. Whether free antivirus software is as good as the commercial alternatives is debatable, but the free antivirus programs are certainly much better than no security software at all. Use a program that runs in the background and provides real-time protection. This software will usually detect and deal with viruses before they have a chance to spread the infection or do any damage to your files.

Backup

Always have at least one backup copy of any important data file. This is not just a matter of having a replacement copy if a file should be destroyed by a virus. The hard disc of a computer has a finite lifespan, and hard disc failures are not a rarity. You should back up all important data anyway, just in case there is a major hard disc failure. It is a good idea to back up the entire system from time to time. This makes it easy to restore a working version of the system, applications programs, etc., in the event of any major problem such as a virus attack, corrupted Windows installation, or hard disc failure.

Windows has included a backup system since the early versions that ran under the MS-DOS operating system. The built-in backup system of the early versions were difficult to use and a bit limited in scope, which meant that few people bothered to use them. The backup software built into recent version of Windows (Figure 1.1) is much easier to use and is also much more sophisticated than the earlier versions. Before buying backup software, or searching the Internet for free software of this type, it is a good idea to investigate the built-in software, which is all that most users will need. The built-in backup software can be accessed via the Backup and Restore section of the Windows Control Panel.

IE settings

In order to make a PC really secure when using the Internet it is necessary to have some hardware and (or) software to protect the system. However, you can improve security by using the computer in the correct manner when online and by having the best settings in Internet Explorer. The settings can be changed by selecting Internet Options from the Tools menu, and then operating the Security tab in the new window that appears (Figure 1.2). The easy way to alter the level of security is to use the slider control near the middle of the window. The higher the setting of this control, the greater the security provided. However, the level of security is increased by disabling various automatic features. With these features disabled it is not possible for an attack site to exploit them, but neither can a site that would make legitimate use of these facilities. Therefore, a high setting will give excellent security, but you will probably find that some web sites no longer work properly with Internet Explorer.

You have to use trial and error to find the highest setting that does not prevent Internet Explorer from working acceptably with the web sites that you use frequently. Of course, it is possible to use one setting for normal Internet use, and a higher one when surfing the Internet and visiting web sites of unknown legitimacy. Changing from one setting to another is quick and easy. No reboot is required, and neither is it necessary to restart Internet Explorer. You do not have to use the preset

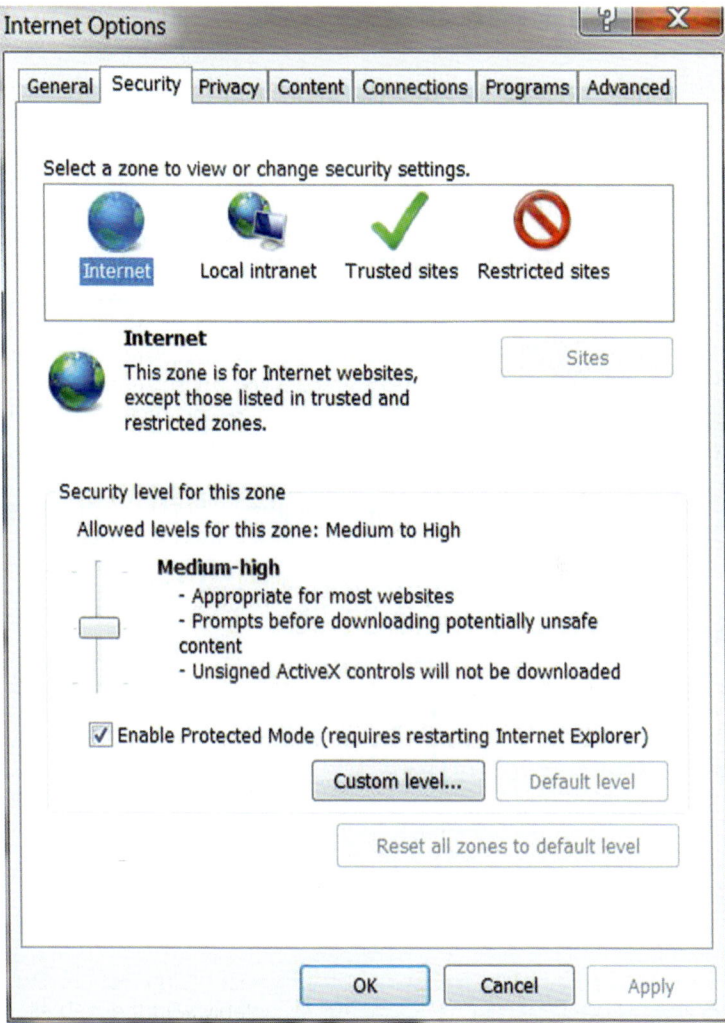

Fig.1.2 The Security section of the Internet Options window

security settings provided by the slider control, and operating the Custom Level button produces a new window where it is possible to individually enable or disable each function (Figure 1.3).

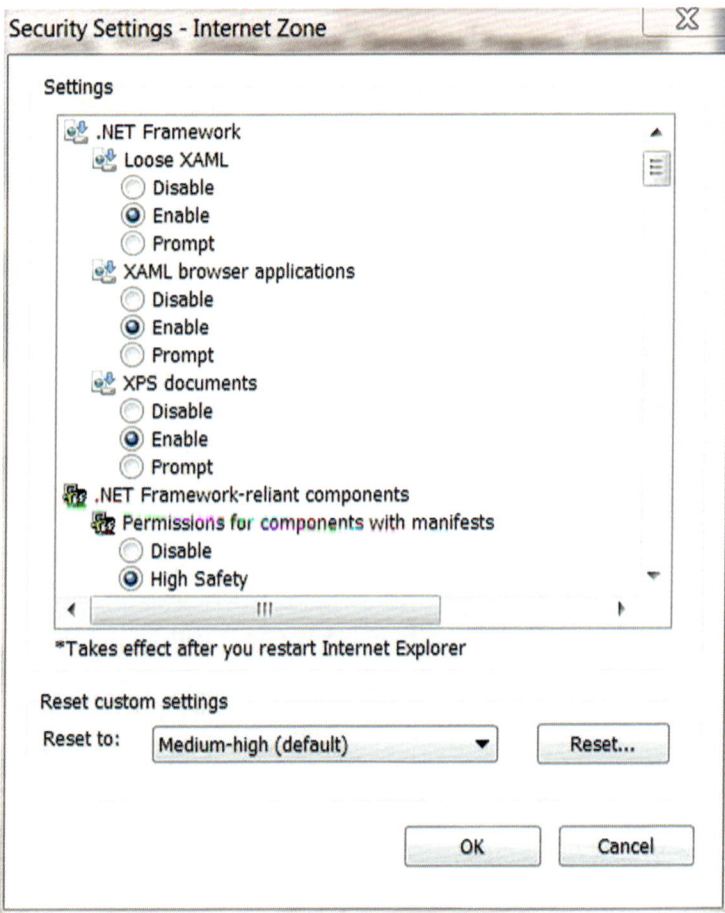

Fig.1.3 Here it is possible to individually switch functions on or off

Privacy settings

There are some useful options available under the Privacy tab (Figure 1.4). The slider in the top section of the window controls cookies, which are text files that are stored on the computer's hard disc drive by some web sites. When visiting some web sites you get a greeting such as "Good morning Bob", and the site knows who you are by consulting the appropriate cookie. While cookies are not generally considered to be a

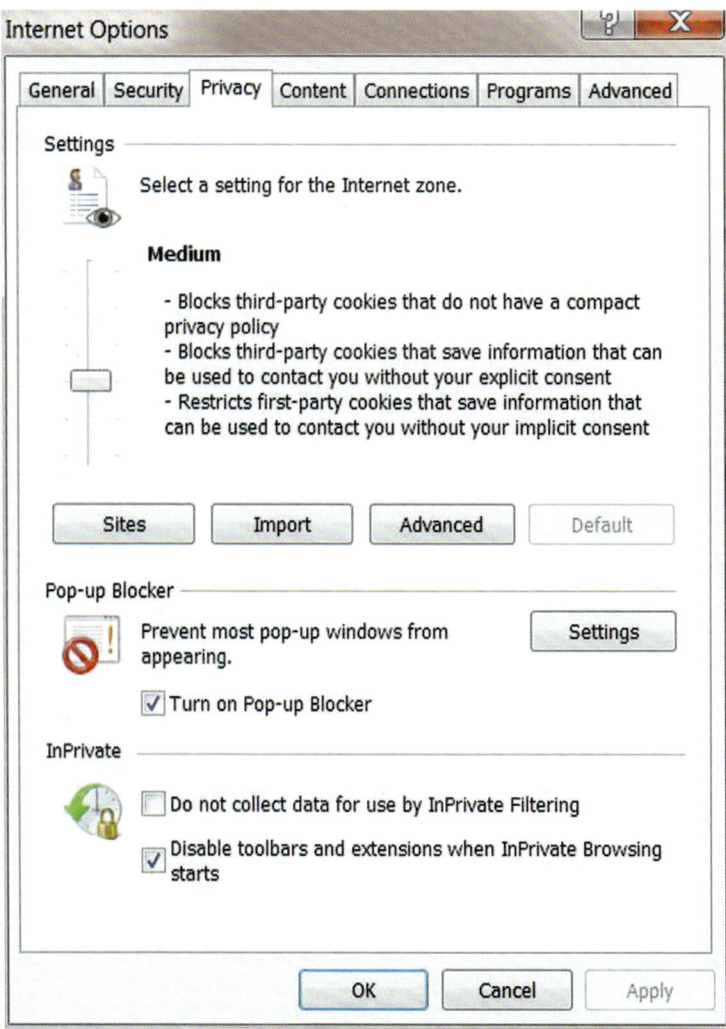

Fig.1.4 The Privacy section of the Internet Options window

major security problem, they do offer a potential means of retrieving personal information from your computer. Simply switching them off altogether removes this security threat, but it is almost certain to result in

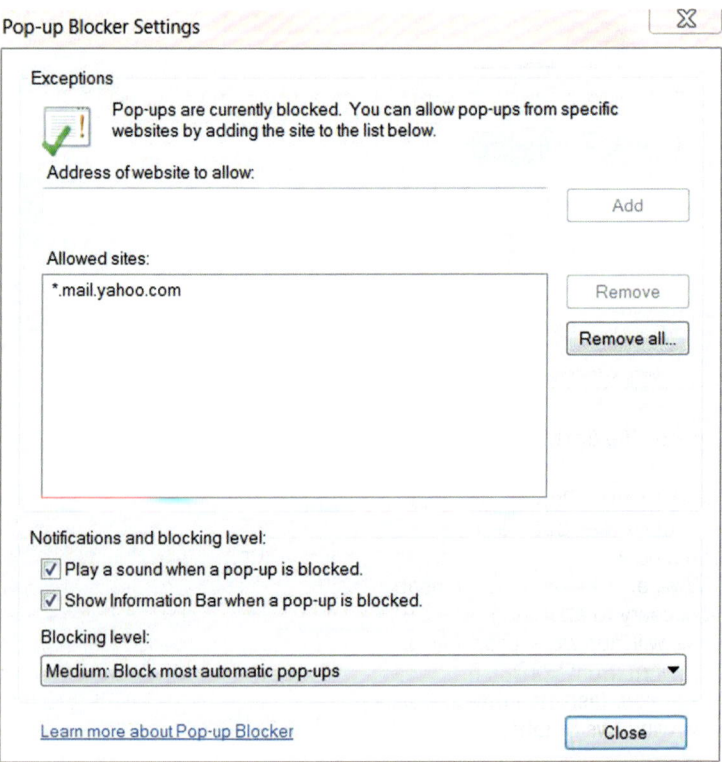

Fig.1.5 Some sites will not work properly unless they are exempted from the Pop-up blocker

some of your favourite web sites failing to work properly. It could make them impossible to use properly, with various clever features failing to work. The setting of the slider control therefore has to be a compromise. The higher the setting that is used, the greater the security obtained, but the greater the likelihood of some web sites not functioning properly. It is a matter of using some trial and error to find the highest setting that does not result in any of your favourite sites being rendered unusable.

Pop-up blocker

The checkbox in the middle section of the window gives the option of using a pop-up blocker, and this will usually be switched on by default. This facility can also be controlled via the Pop-up Blocker entry in the

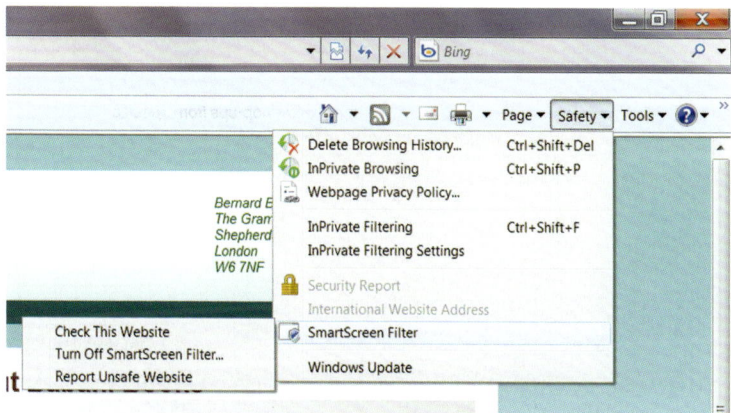

Fig.1.6 The SmartScreen filtering can be switched on or off

Tools menu. Pop-up advertisements are more of a nuisance than a security threat, but they do represent a potential means of automatically directing your computer to a site that will try to infect it with some sort of malware. Anyway, it is advisable to use this option. It is not usually necessary to alter the Pop-up Blocker's settings (Figure 1.5), but some sites will not work properly unless they are exempted from pop-up blocking. Some online Email services for example, might only operate in a limited fashion if the Pop-up Blocker prevents them from launching new windows or tabs.

Phishing filter

Some browsers now have a phishing filter, which is a feature that blocks access and warns you if the selected web page is part of a known phishing site. It would be a mistake to rely totally on a feature such as this, since it can only warn you about sites that have been reported and found to be genuine fakes. It will not block phishing sites that are very new and have not yet been reported and checked. You still have to use some common sense and try to spot phishing sites yourself. However, it is clearly a good idea to use any feature of this type, which might prevent you from doing something silly. It is also a good idea to make use of any other feature that blocks the browser from entering other forms of malicious web site.

Internet Explorer 7 and 8 both have a phishing filter, and this is normally activated by default. In Internet Explorer 8 it is part of the SmartScreen

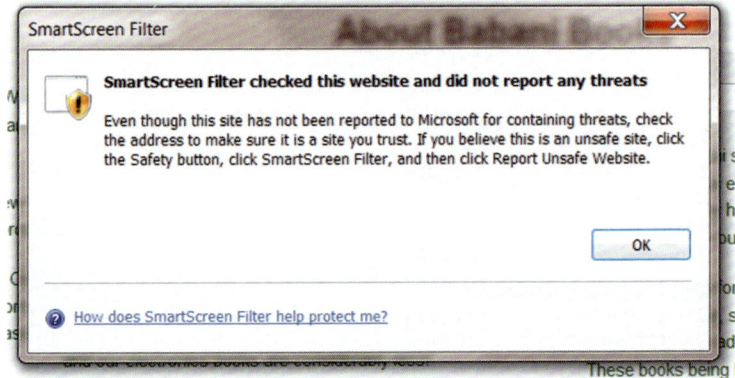

Fig.1.7 The current page can be checked for security threats

Filter, and it can be switched on and off via SmartScreen entry in the Tools menu (Figure 1.6). With Internet Explorer 7 you have to choose Tools, then Phishing Filter, and finally Phishing Filter Settings. It can then be switched on or off using the Disable Phishing Filter radio button. In Internet Explorer the SmartScreen menu entry includes a facility for checking the current page for potential threats. No threats have been detected in the example scan of Figure 1.7. Some security suites offer similar facilities, and it is advisable to stay away from any page that is flagged as a possible security threat.

Mystery files

Be very careful if you find a file on your PC and you do not know what it is or how it found its way onto the hard disc. Opening some form of document file (PDF, DOC, and so on) or running some form of program file (EXE or COM) could activate some form of attack. Simply deleting a mystery file is not a good idea because it might be a file you need but have forgotten about. It is better to first copy the file to a floppy disc, CD/RW, Flash memory card, or whatever, and then delete the original. The normal Delete function of Windows puts erased files in the Recycle Bin rather than deleting them straight away. This could leave a Trojan or similar file still on the hard disc. In order to genuinely delete a file it is first selected using Windows Explorer, and then the Delete key is pressed while holding down the Shift key. The file will appear to have been deleted in the normal way, but it will be conspicuously absent from the Recycle Bin.

Keep up-to-date

Many viruses and worms are designed to exploit a security flaw in an applications program or the operating system itself. Sometimes these flaws have already been covered by software updates, but not everyone has bothered to update their PCs and the infection is able to spread. In fairness to amateur PC users, there have been worms that have exploited old security "holes" in the operating systems of servers. The professionals maintaining the affected servers had not bothered to routinely update their systems, leaving them vulnerable to attack from what should have been obsolete malware. Some worms and viruses exploit previously unknown security flaws, but patches to fix the problem are soon made available when this sort of thing occurs. You would be very unlucky indeed to become a victim of one of these provided you always install new security updates for the operating system.

Some applications programs now have an automatic update facility, as does the Windows operating system. A system such as this could be regarded as a potential security risk itself, but manual updates are usually available from the software publisher's web site if you do not trust the automatic approach. Make sure that you use one or the other, and this is especially important for browsers and programs that support some form of programming language, macro language, scripts or anything of this general type.

Firewalls

Although some people seem to think that a firewall and antivirus programs are the same, there are major differences between the two. There is often some overlap between real world antivirus and firewall programs, but their primary aims are completely different. An antivirus program is designed to scan files on discs and the contents of the computer's memory in search of viruses and other potentially harmful files. Having found any suspect files, the program will usually deal with them. A firewall is used to block access to your PC, and in most cases it is access to your PC via the Internet that is blocked. Bear in mind though, that a software firewall will usually block access via a local area network (LAN) as well. Of course, a firewall is of no practical value if it blocks communication from one PC to another and access via the Internet. What it is actually doing is keeping hackers at bay by preventing unauthorised access to the protected PC. When you access an Internet site your PC sends messages to the server hosting that site, and these messages request the pages you wish to view. Having requested information, the PC expects information to be sent from the appropriate server, and it accepts that information when it is received. A firewall does not interfere with this type of Internet activity provided it is set up correctly.

It is a different matter when another system tries to access your PC when you have not instigated the initial contact. The firewall will treat this attempted entry as an attack and will block it. Of course, the attempt at accessing your PC might not be an attack, and a firewall can result in legitimate access being blocked. An application such as P2P file sharing is likely to fail or operate in a limited fashion. The sharing of files and resources on a local area network could also be blocked.

A practical firewall enables the user to permit certain types of access so that the computer can work normally while most unauthorised access is still blocked. However, doing so does reduce the degree of protection provided by the firewall. Recent versions of Windows come complete with a basic firewall program that is enabled by default. There are plenty of commercial firewall programs that can be used instead if you feel that a more sophisticated Firewall program would be desirable. Of more relevance in the current context, there are several free firewall programs that are very effective. Note that some broadband routers have a built-in firewall, but the capabilities of these facilities vary considerably. Using a free firewall program is covered in Chapter 3 and will not be considered further here.

Digital certificates

Digital certificates are something that you are likely to encounter on the Internet from time to time. The purpose of the certificate is to guarantee the identity of an individual or organisation, and they could be regarded as the digital version of a passport. Having the identity of the person or organisation properly verified should in turn guarantee that you can safely download their program, use their site or whatever. Typically a digital certificate is encountered when downloading a player program to permit a media file to be played. Digital certificates are also much used for secure web sites.

In order to be of any value the certificate must be issued by a recognised certificate authority (CA) such as VeriSign. Certificates have an expiry date and must be renewed from time to time. Occasionally a warning message might be produced as you enter a site, due to the certificate having been allowed to lapse. There is probably nothing to worry about if the site is one that is tried and tested. The certificate has probably been allowed to lapse due to an oversight. If the site is not one that you have used regularly in the past it is probably a good idea to give it a miss until the certificate is renewed.

Secure site?

Many web sites claim that they are secure and that any information that you supply to them is hacker-proof, but how do you know if a site is actually a secure type? For that matter, what exactly is a secure site? Sites that take sensitive information such as credit card details normally use encryption so that your information is safe from hackers. A hacker might actually intercept the information, but as it is encrypted it is not in a form that is of any use to them. Even using the most powerful computers available today it would take many years to "crack" the code and extract your credit card details or whatever. No one is going to bother, and the information would probably be well out of date by the time it was recovered by a hacker.

By default, Internet Explorer will tell you when you are entering and leaving a secure site. This can get a bit irritating, so most users switch off these messages. Even where they are still operational, it can be difficult to keep track of things if the messages keep popping up. Fortunately it is very easy to determine whether or not a secure site is being accessed using Internet Explorer. A tiny padlock icon appears near the bottom right-hand corner of the window when visiting a secure site using one of the older versions of Internet Explorer. If this icon is absent, the site is not secure, even it contains claims to the contrary. With later versions the address bar goes green when visiting a secure site. Again, the site is not a secure type if this fails to happen. Most other browsers use a similar system.

Windows Defender

Modern versions of Windows come complete with a program called Windows Defender, which is primarily designed to counter spyware and pop-up advertisements on web pages. It is definitely not intended to be a complete solution to problems with malicious software, and it should be used in addition to antivirus software rather than instead of it. Windows Defender is considered in more detail in the next chapter.

Stealth malware

A final but important point is that many people still think that most computer infections are of the old virus type, and that their presence will soon become apparent as they start to attack the computer system. This type of malware is still in circulation, and I am still asked to deal with this type of thing from time to time. However, the traditional computer virus only accounts for a few percent of computer infections. Most of the malware currently in circulation is of the so-called "stealth" variety. Far from making obvious attacks on the system, it is carefully designed to remain undetected for as long as possible.

The practical consequence of this is that it is no use waiting until your computer shows obvious signs of an infection before taking any security measures. Handling things in this fashion could result in your computer being used to steal your personal information for a long period of time before you realise that something is amiss. These days it is essential to have security software running on your PC and protecting it against attacks. Even if you do not notice anything out of the ordinary, good security software should soon detect any malware on your computer. In fact it may even detect and block it, thus preventing your computer from becoming infected in the first place.

Free antivirus software

Up-to-date

If you use the Internet, these days it is essential to have an antivirus program that provides real-time protection. This does not guarantee that viruses will be blocked from your PC, but it greatly reduces the risk of infection. If the worst should happen, in order to permanently remove most modern computer infections it is necessary to use an up-to-date antivirus program. As pointed out in chapter 1, new PCs are almost

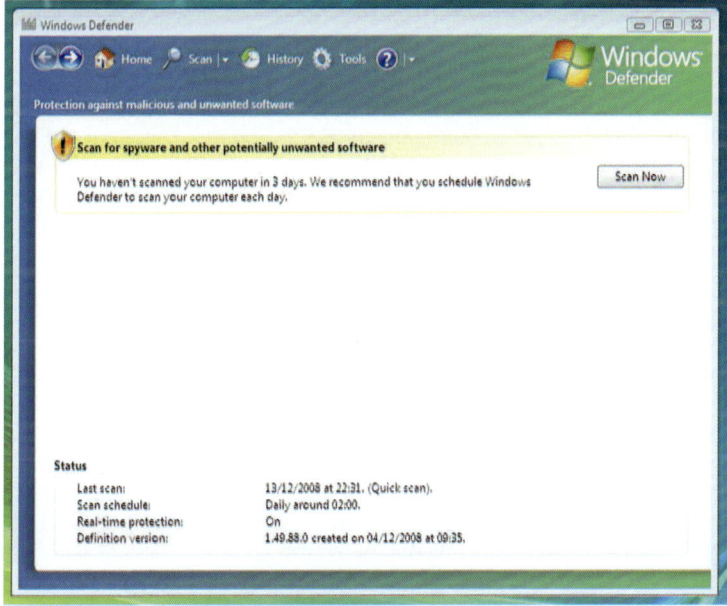

Fig.2.1 The Windows Defender information window

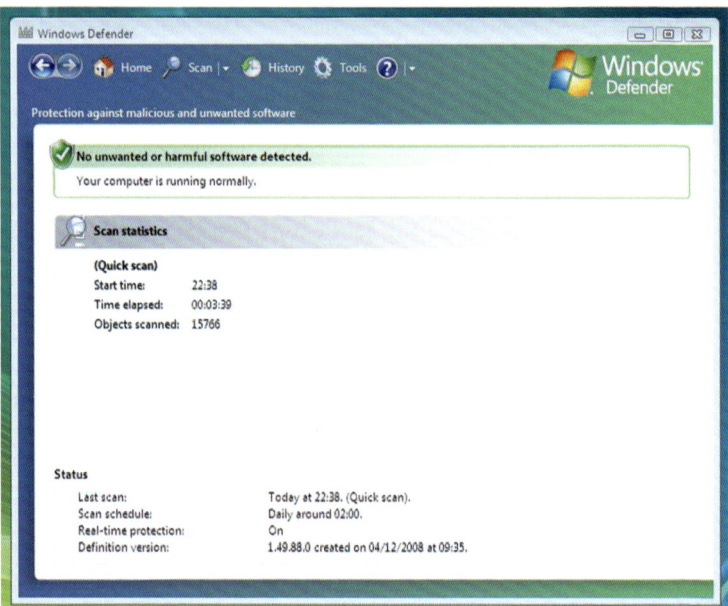

Fig.2.2 In this example no threats were found

invariably supplied complete with a commercial antivirus program, but this usually has a fairly short subscription to updates. After a month or three the virus database is no longer updated with details of new viruses, and the program then becomes less and less effective with the passage of time. An out-of-date antivirus program is better than nothing, but it will be far less than one hundred percent effective.

Windows Defender

There are better ways of handling things than continuing to use a commercial antivirus program that is relying on out-of-date virus definitions. As mentioned in the previous chapter, Windows 7 and Vista have a built-in program that is designed to protect the computer from various types of threat, and it is called Windows Defender. This is normally included as part of a standard Windows 7 and Vista installation, so it will almost certainly run automatically each time your computer is switched on.

Windows Defender runs in the background, protecting your computer all the time it is switched on. The main program can be accessed by

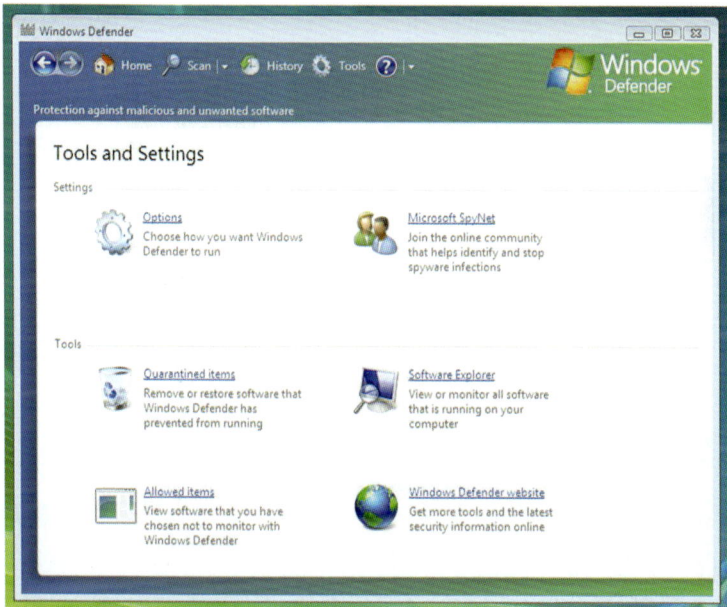

Fig.2.3 Operate the options button

going to the Start menu, selecting All Programs, and then choosing Windows Defender from the menu. This produces a window like the one shown in Figure 2.1, which provides information about the last time that Windows Defender did a scan of the system. A scan can be started manually by operating the Scan Now button, and in due course this will provide the scan results. No threats were found in the example of Figure 2.2, and therefore none were removed from the system.

Note that Windows Defender will almost certainly be switched off if there is another anti-spyware program running on the computer. With any real-time security software there should only be one program of a given type running at any one time. There is otherwise a risk of the two programs interacting in a way that makes them less effective, and there is also a risk of the computer crashing. In general, it is all right if there is a real-time security program running at the same time as another program scans the system for infected files or other threats. The two programs will be providing different functions, and there will be little risk of conflicts arising. With two real-time programs of a similar type there will almost certainly be conflicts and problems.

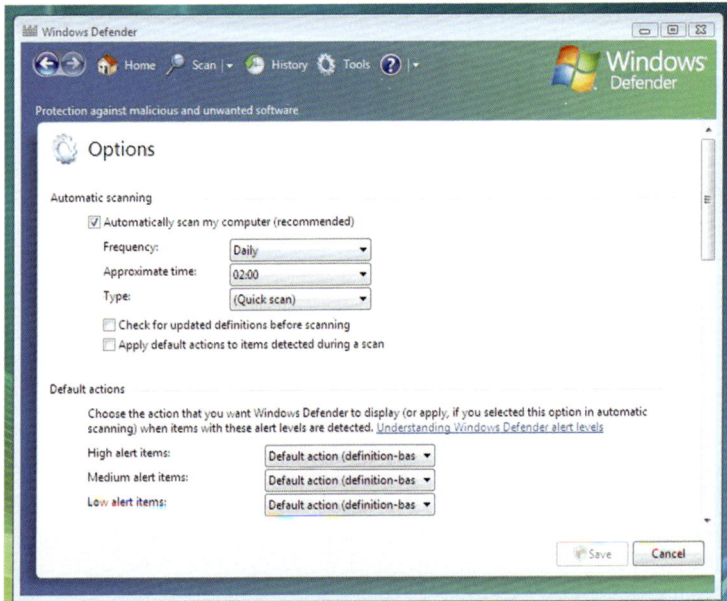

Fig.2.4 The time at which scanning takes place can be changed

In control

It is possible to control the way in which Windows Defender operates by first left-clicking the Tools icon near the top of the window, which changes it to look like Figure 2.3. Next operate the Options button, and the window will then change to the one shown in Figure 2.4. There are various parameters that can be altered here, but in most cases the default settings will suffice. However, you might like to alter the time at which automatic scanning takes place. The default is usually for this to occur at about 2:00 in the morning, when it is unlikely that your computer will be running. A more suitable time can then be selected from the pop-down menu.

As with most software of this general type, the program can undertake a quick scan or a more thorough type. Obviously a thorough scan is preferable, but each scan of this type can take a very long time. In fact with many PCs it takes too long to be practical for daily scanning. Quick scanning is then the more practical choice, perhaps with the occasional full scan started manually. Of course, it is not necessary to have a daily scan at all, and one of the menus offers scans at other intervals. The scanning can be switched off completely by removing the tick in the "Automatically scan my computer" checkbox.

Online antivirus

Windows Defender is primarily designed to counter spyware and pop-up advertisements on web pages, and it is not intended to be a complete solution to problems with malicious software. It should be used in addition to antivirus software rather than instead of it. If you do not wish to pay for a subscription to commercial antivirus software there are some good free alternatives available.

One option is to use a free online virus checking facility to periodically scan your PC, but the drawback of this method is that there is no real-time protection for your PC. By the time you do a virus scan it is possible that a virus could have been spreading across your files for some time. By the time it is detected and removed it is likely that a significant amount of damage would already have been done.

An antivirus program running on your PC will, like Windows Defender, provide real-time protection. In other words, it monitors disc drive activity, Internet activity, or anything that might involve a virus or other malicious program. If any suspicious files are detected, there is an attempt to alter system files, or any dubious activity is detected, the user is warned. In most cases the virus or other malicious program is blocked or removed from the system before it has a chance to do any harm.

This is not to say that online virus scanning systems are of no value at all. They can be useful when used in addition to a real-time system. With a continuous stream of new malicious software it is not possible for any antivirus program to give guaranteed protection against every threat. Using an online virus scanner gives a "second opinion", and increases the chances of finding any malware that has infected your computer. In fact there is something to be said for using several of these scanners from time-to-time, or if you have reason to believe that your PC might be infected.

Of course, there is a drawback to using an online antivirus scanner once an infection has occurred. Your PC must be largely operational before it can go online and be used with this type of scanning. The same is true of a scanner program running on your PC. These days the majority of malware does not actually try to bring the infected PC to a halt. Most malware is intended to steal information from the infected PC, or to make it easy for a hacker to take it over and use it for dubious or illegal purposes. Computers in this second category are known as "robots", or just "bots", and they can be used to send spam Emails or as part of a DOS (denial of service) attack. Some malware causes the default Internet browser to be launched and directed to a certain web site or site.

The important point here is that in each case the malware does not try to stop the PC from functioning, and it actually needs the computer to be in fully operational condition with a working Internet connection. Thus in most cases there is no problem if you try to use an online antivirus scanner, or a facility of this type that is part of your normal security software. However, you need to be aware that some malware will block access to well known security sites and might also try to prevent any installed security software from functioning properly. It can be difficult to remove malware when the degree of infection has reached this sort of level, and reinstalling everything from scratch might then be the most practical solution.

Potential flaws

There are various companies that offer online virus scanning facilities, and most of these are free. The name suggests that a program running at the server scans your PC for viruses, but in most cases very little of the software runs at the other end of the Internet link. The usual arrangement is for an antivirus program to be downloaded to your PC, temporarily installed, run and then erased. In some cases the program is an ordinary Windows type, but it is more usually in the form of an ActiveX control or an applet of some kind. It will not always be automatically erased, and if you prefer not to leave it on the system it might be necessary to go to the Windows Control Panel and erase it in the normal way.

A potential problem with the online scanning method is that it is not really much different to installing an antivirus program and running it in the usual way. In most cases that is basically what you are doing when using one of these facilities. The potential problem is that the file copying provides opportunities for any virus to propagate, and going online provides spyware and backdoor Trojans with an opportunity to "do their thing". It is better to plan ahead and already have an up-to-date antivirus scanning program installed on your PC.

If you suspect that there could be a problem with a virus but have no definite proof, then it might be worth the risk if you do not have a better alternative. Online testing is also worthwhile if you do not intend to use

Fig.2.5 The Panda Software homepage for UK users

normal antivirus software, but it has to be emphasised that it is certainly not a genuine alternative to normal antivirus software. One of the better free antivirus programs such as AVG Free will monitor your PC and provide real-time protection. Any virus entering the system is likely to be detected immediately. With occasional online scanning there could be a significant gap between the infection occurring and the virus being detected. Even a few days or hours could be long enough for the virus to spread and damage your files.

A program such as AVG free will provide a scanning facility in addition to real-time protection, so you can easily scan the system if you suspect that an infection has penetrated the real-time protection. I suppose online testing might be worthwhile if you are at the stage where you are desperate enough to try anything, but as far as possible it is best to avoid getting into that situation. Installing free antivirus software on your PC is far better than getting into difficulties and then trying to recover the situation.

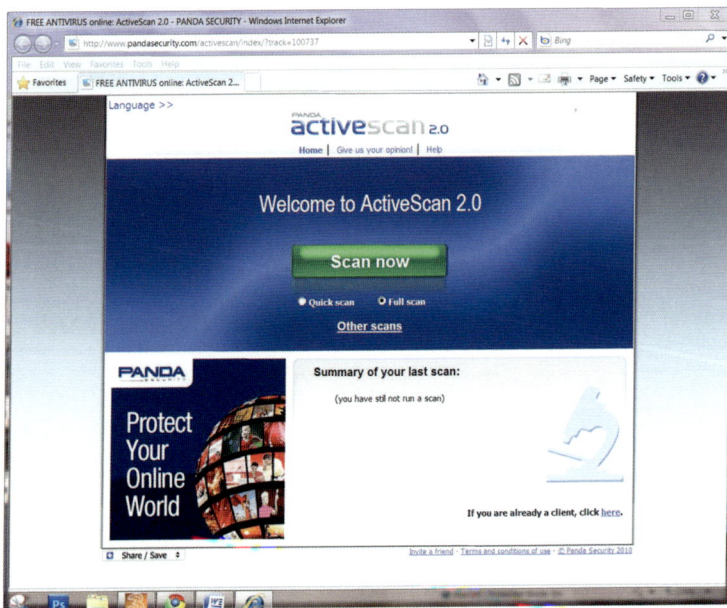

Fig.2.6 The page provides a summary of any previous scan

Go carefully

An important point if you do try online virus scanning is to make sure that you use the services of a reputable company. In the early days of computer viruses it was quite common for infections to be spread via antivirus software that was actually a Trojan. This method has rather gone out of fashion, but the possibility of someone coming up with an online version cannot be ruled out. Only using the services of a "big name" company should ensure that the scanning detects and removes any viruses rather than adding a few! This advice should be heeded when downloading any free software, and it is best not to download anything from a website of unknown pedigree.

Panda software

Panda Software is well known for its security oriented software suites, and they offer online scanning in the form of the ActiveScan facility. The

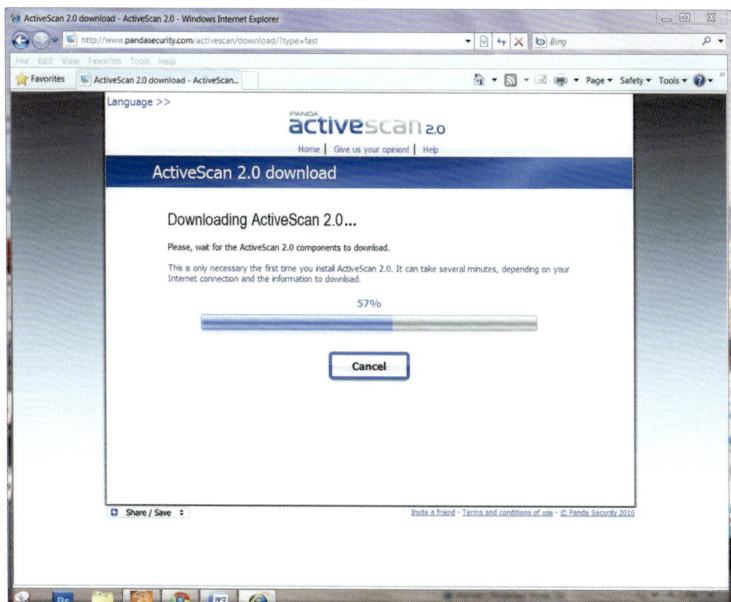

Fig.2.7 The online scan requires a file to be downloaded

Panda software homepage for the United Kingdom is shown in Figure 2.5, and is available at:

www.pandasecurity.com/uk

Operating the Scan Your PC link near the top left-hand corner of the page brings up the initial window of Figure 2.6, which will give a summary of the previous scan, if there was one. The bottom section of the page will be blank when using ActiveScan for the first time, as in this example.

There are two radio buttons that provide the options of a full scan or a quick scan. It is quite common for antivirus programs to offer a choice of this type, and the reason for offering a quick scan is that a full type can take quite a lot of time. A comprehensive scan of a computer that has two large hard disc drives that each contains many thousands of files could take several hours. Incidentally, if your PC is used in conjunction with an external hard disc drive, as many are these days, it is advisable to have the external hard disc connected to the PC and included in any scan for viruses or other malware. Although it could be very time consuming, always opt for a full scan if you have reason to suspect that your computer is infected.

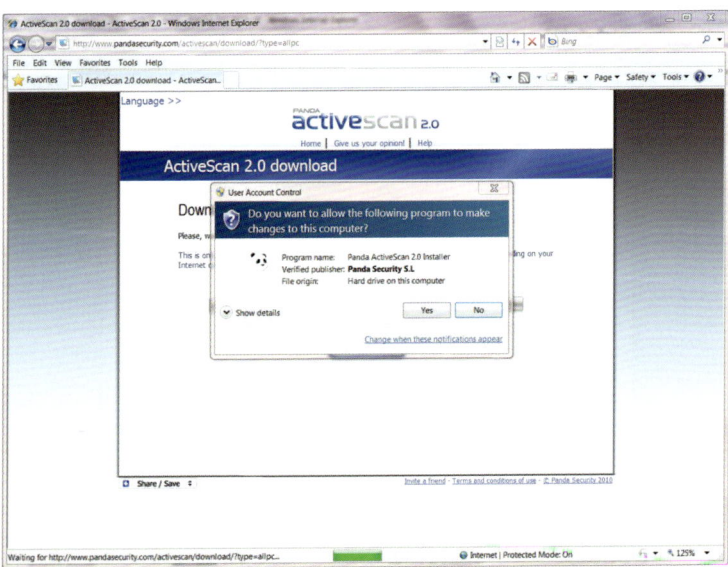

Fig.2.8 Operate the Yes button to go ahead and run the software

Operating the Scan Now button moves things on to the window of Figure 2.7 where the download process begins. As pointed out previously, online scans are largely performed by software on your computer rather than a program running on a remote server, so the program file has to be downloaded before scanning can commence. Depending on the version of Windows you are using, there might be various warning messages about the dangers of downloading software. There will be at least one of these with any reasonably modern version of Windows (Figure 2.8). If any messages of this type appear, indicate that you wish to proceed with the download.

Having downloaded the program file you will probably have to download an update in order to proceed. This might include an update to the program itself, but in most cases it is actually the latest database of virus definitions that is being downloaded. It is essential that an up-to-date set of virus definitions is used, so any available updates should always be installed before scanning for malware.

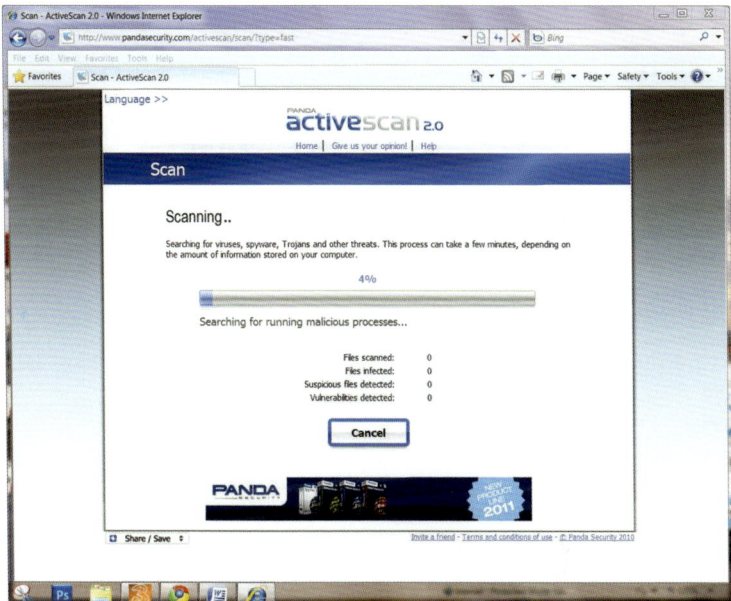

Fig.2.9 The scan in under way, and this window shows how things are progressing

Registration

Often when downloading free software it is necessary to provide a valid Email address or go through some form of registration process. This is not currently the case with Panda Software's ActiveScan. In cases where an Email address is required it is not essential to use your normal Email address, and any valid address can be used. If you do not wish to use your normal Email address for this type of thing it is just a matter of setting up an account with Hotmail, Yahoo, or one of the other online Email providers. This account can then be used when obtaining free online services, which almost invariably require a valid Email address. Where there is a registration process that requires a lot of personal information it is probably best to abort the process and look for alternative software.

Another warning message will probably appear once the scanning program is ready to run, and the Yes button must be operated in order to proceed. A window like the one in Figure 2.9 is produced once all the

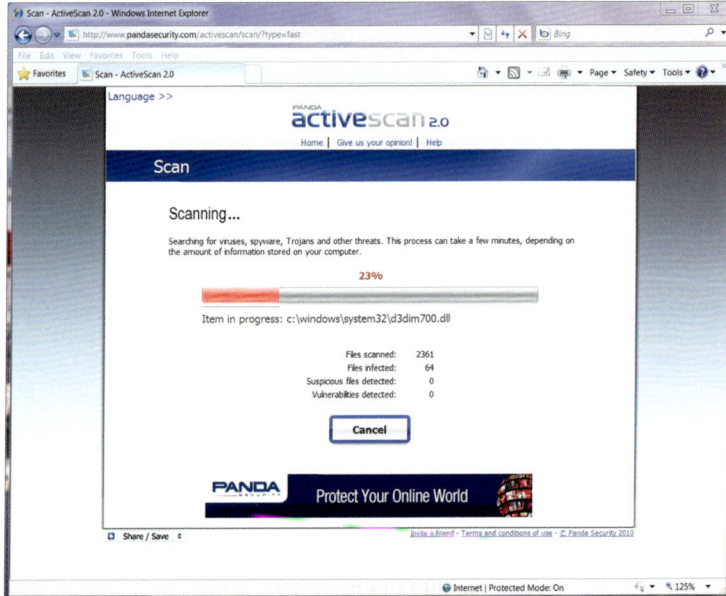

Fig.2.10 Some threats have been detected

preliminaries have been completed and scan is under way. This has a bargraph display to show how far the scan has progressed. A table of results is included, and this shows things like the number of files tested, and any actions taken by the program. Note that it is not necessary to remain online while the scanning takes place, but that the PC must be online before the final results can be produced. The table of results is updated to show any suspicious files or registry entries that are found (Figure 2.10). As with any antivirus scanning, it can take some time if there is a large and largely full hard disc drive to check. Eventually the scan will be completed though and a full set of results will then be shown (Figure 2.11).

The program is much like an ordinary antivirus program in operation, and this is essentially what it is. However, when you exit the program it will effectively be uninstalled, and it cannot be run in the usual fashion. In order to use the program again it is necessary to go back online and go through this process again. Although a number of infections have been located in this case, they are all in the form of tracking cookies, which are not generally considered to be a major security risk. Many

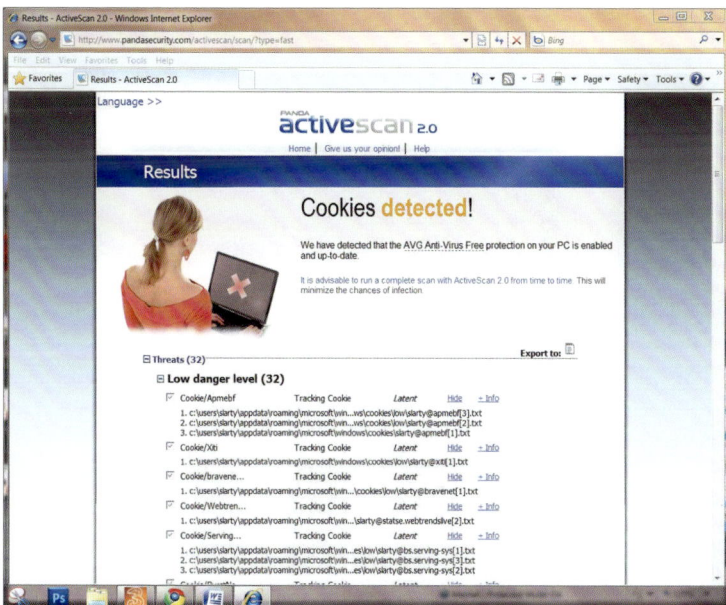

*Fig.2.11 The scan has been completed, and the full set of results are
shown*

scanning programs will simply ignore objects of this type. They are
perhaps an invasion of privacy rather than a genuine security risk, but
many people prefer to have them erased.

There are other types of scan available via the Other Scans link on the
initial ActiveScan page (Figure 2.6). Using this option produces the
screen of Figure 2.12 where three more options are available. The one
at the top is used if you just wish to scan your documents for possible
threats. The middle option is used if you wish to scan your Emails for
infections, and this is a facility that is now offered by most antivirus
software. Bear in mind though, that features of this type are dependent
on the right type of Email service being used. In general Email scanners
either fail to work at all with online Email services or are of limited value.
Since online Email services such as Yahoo Mail and Microsoft's Hotmail
have built-in virus scanning there is probably little point in using your
own scanning software with them. Any threats should have already been
detected and dealt with by the time the Emails reach your computer's
Email scanner.

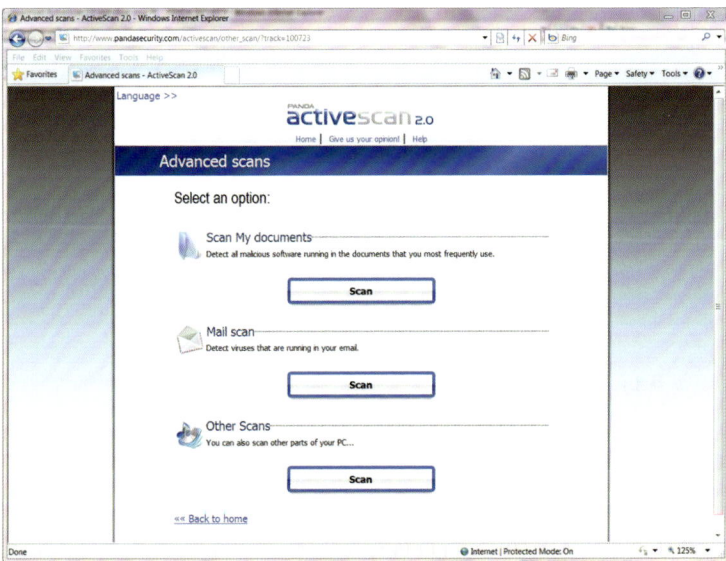

Fig.2.12 Various scanning options are available

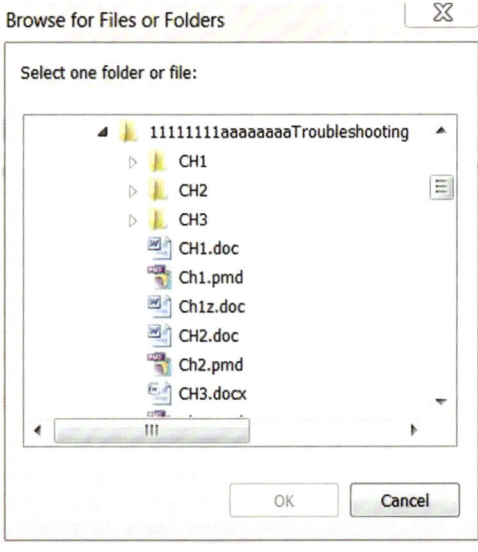

Fig.2.13 Select the required files or folders

The Other Scans option is used if you wish to scan only a certain part or certain areas of your computer. Selecting this option produces the usual file and folder browser (Figure 2.13) where the required parts of the computer's file system can be selected in the standard way. Thereafter, the scanning process proceeds in the same way as before.

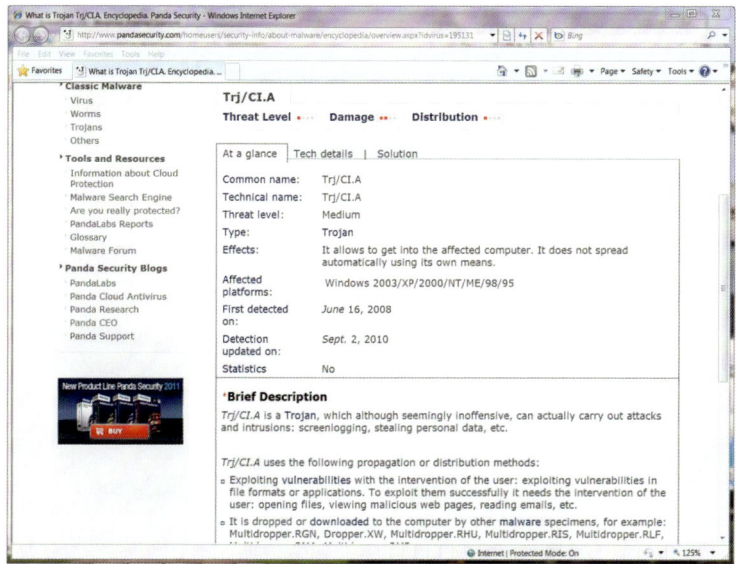

Fig.2.14 Information is available for reported infections

Beyond scanning

A point to bear in mind with online virus scanners is that most of them are simply that. They scan for potential problems and report anything suspicious that is located. They do not actually remove anything that is found, and it is up to the user to delete files or make any other changes that are required. Panda Software's ActiveScan used to have a facility for removing infected files, but this does not seem to be a feature of the current free online version. It points out suspected problems, and by operating the relevant link in the scan report it is possible to obtain more information about the detected infection (Figure 2.14). There is no help beyond that, and it is up to the user to investigate matters further and manually remove the infection. In some cases this merely entails deleting the infected file or files, but in other cases it is significantly more complex than that.

BitDefender is one of the few online scanners that will also try to remove any infections that are found. The homepage for the free online version is here (Figure 2.15):

www.bitdefender.com/scanner/online/free.html

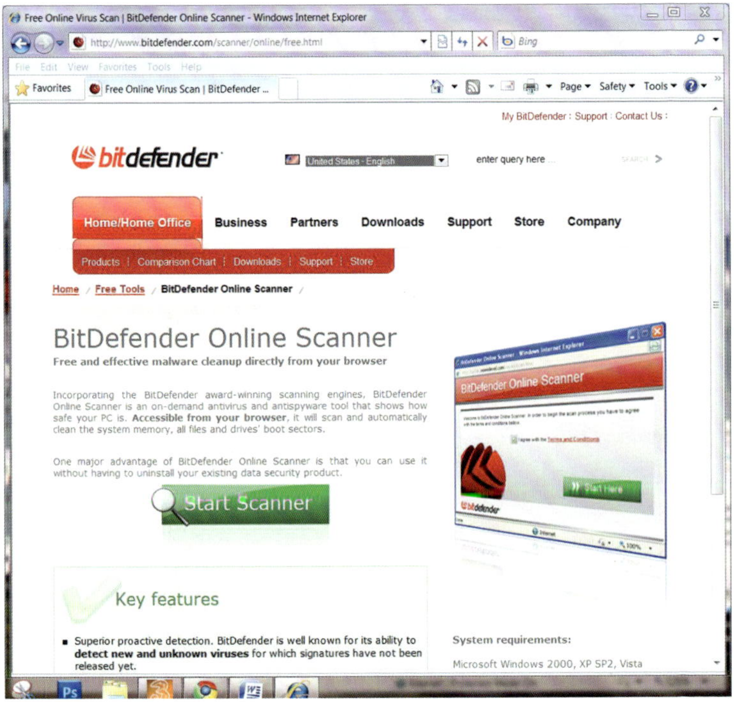

Fig.2.15 The BitDefender homepage

Fig.2.16 You have to agree to their terms and conditions

Operating the Start Scanner button produces the window of Figure 2.16, where you have to tick the checkbox to agree to the terms and conditions, and then operate the Start Here button in order to proceed. The message window of Figure 2.17 then appears, and this informs you that the scanner software is being downloaded. As usual, it is necessary to confirm that you wish to continue if any warning messages pop up on the screen.

Fig.2.17 The software is being downloaded

An error message appeared when I tried this scanner for the first time. The gist of the message was that the scanner would not be able to operate properly because Internet Explorer is not being run with administrator privileges. Most online scanners are not totally independent pieces of software, and are reliant on a web browser. In some cases it must be the right web browser program, which usually means a recent version of Internet Explorer, but some will also operate with one or two alternatives such as Firefox or Chrome. Simply using the right web browser might not be enough, and in some instances, as here, the browser's settings and operating conditions must be right as well. In this example I had to start again from the beginning, switching off Internet Explorer and running it again with administrator privileges. In order to do this it is just a matter of right-clicking on the icon or menu entry used to launch Internet Explorer, and then selecting "Run as administrator" from the pop-up menu (Figure 2.18).

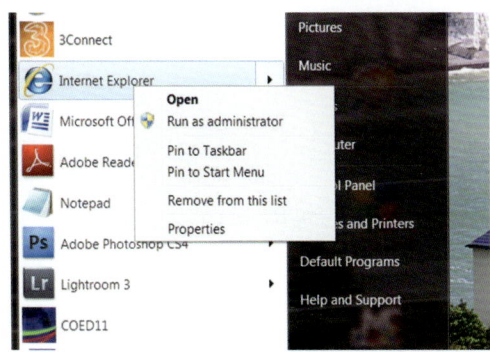

Fig.2.18 Run Internet Explorer as an administrator

Things proceeded properly with Internet Explorer running in the correct mode, and the window of Figure 2.19 eventually appeared. It is not

Fig.2.19 The defaults will usually suffice, but settings can be changed here

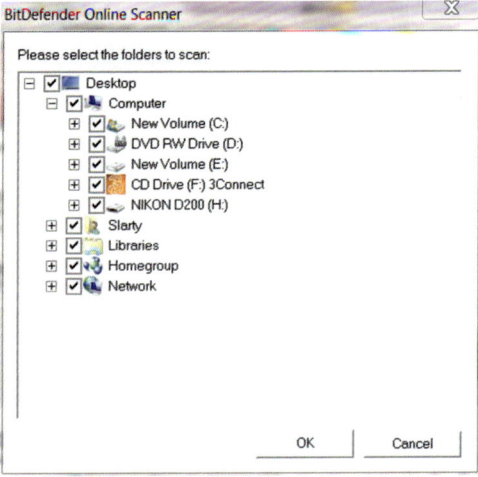

Fig.2.20 Select the folders to be scanned

essential to alter any settings, and using the defaults results in the entire computer being scanned. The program will try to fix any problems that are found, in addition to reporting them of course. The parts of the computer to be scanned can be selected using the Folders to Scan link, which produces the pop-up browser of Figure 2.20. This is a folder browser rather than a file browser, so you can select folders and subfolders, but not individual files. If you wish to check the settings or make changes, operating the Cleaning Options link produces the pop-up window of Figure 2.21. Here there are options that enable the user to select the types of detection used, and the action or actions to be taken when a suspected infection is found.

Heuristic scanning

Some virus scanning programs, including BitDefender, can provide heuristic scanning, and this is an option in the Cleaning Options window.

Heuristic scanning is a technique of looking for files that have the characteristics of viruses, but do not exactly match any entries in the virus database. The advantage of the heuristic approach is that it does not leave you perpetually one step behind the virus writers. Most viruses are actually just minor variations on those already in existence, but a normal matching process will

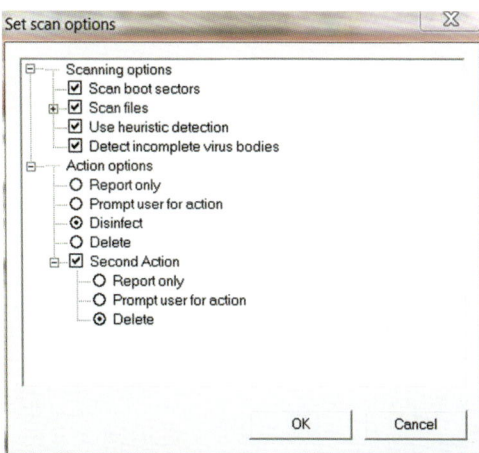

Fig.2.21 Select the required types of scanning

not detect them. The new viruses are similar to existing ones, but are sufficiently different to prevent a match from being obtained. Writers of malicious software deliberately make frequent but quite minor changes to their programs in an attempt to defeat antivirus programs.

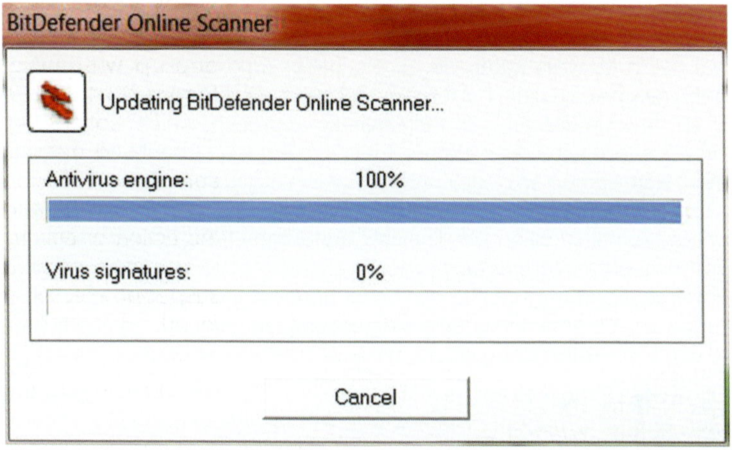

Fig.2.22 The program will be updated before scanning commences

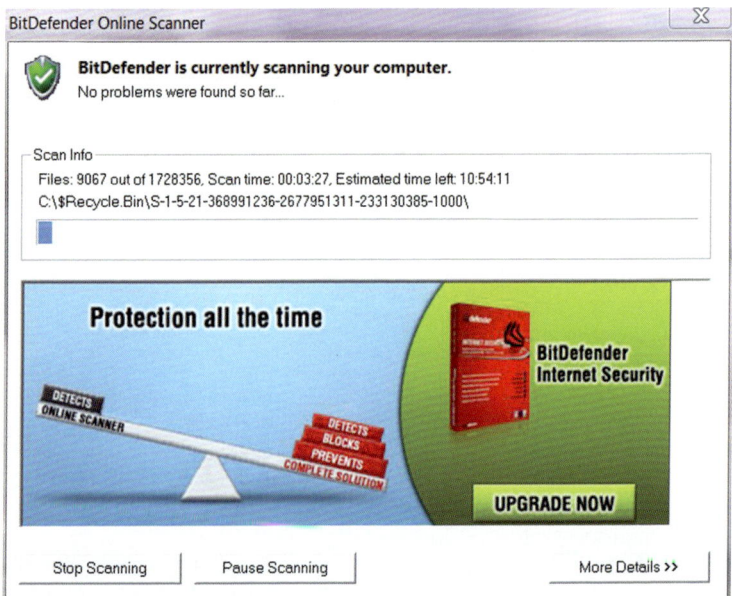

Fig.2.23 The scanning process is under way

A heuristic approach is more likely to find these variations since it is looking for certain tell-tale pieces of code rather than a perfect match overall. Potentially, the heuristic approach can find new viruses that are not yet in its virus database, giving better protection. It will not find genuinely new viruses, but it will detect most of the recycled ones. There is an obvious danger with the heuristic approach, which is that it will produce too many false alarms if it is applied too strongly. In the past there were sometimes major problems with antivirus programs producing large numbers of so-called "false positives". Some antivirus software offered something along the lines of Careful and Strong heuristic settings, and in most cases it was best to opt for the more cautious setting. Modern antivirus programs seem to use better heuristic techniques that are less prone to problems with spurious detections. Anyway, it is generally best to use a heuristic option where this is offered as an option.

Once everything is to your satisfaction it is just a matter of operating the Start Scanning button. There will be the inevitable updating process (Figure 2.22), and the scanning process will then commence (Figure 2.23). The program gives details of the progress made, and any malicious

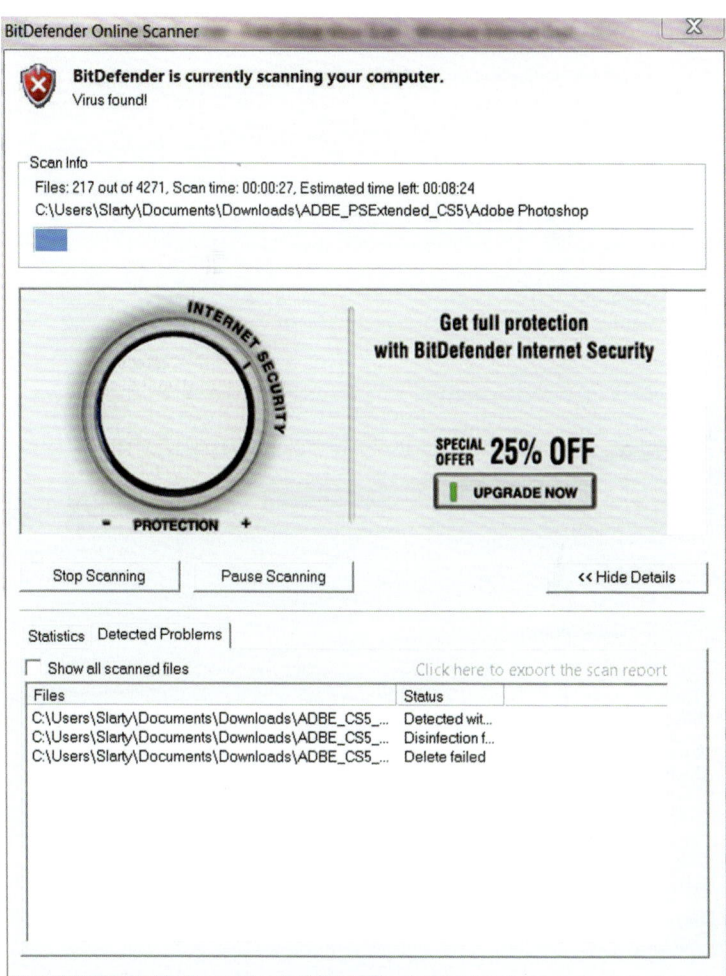

*Fig.2.24 The lower section of the window shows any threats
          detected and the actions taken*

objects found will be listed in the lower section of the window (Figure
2.24). Details of any actions taken will also be given here. Eventually
the scanning will be completed (Figure 2.25), but it can take several
hours in order to scan a computer that has one or two large hard disc
drives that contain vast numbers of files.

Fig.2.25 The scanning and cleaning process has been completed

Two infected objects have been found in this example, and these are two dubious files that I downloaded and left on the hard disc drive for BitDefender to find. The reason it has not been able to remove the infections or delete the infected files is that both files are part of a compressed archive file. It would be possible to decompress the archives

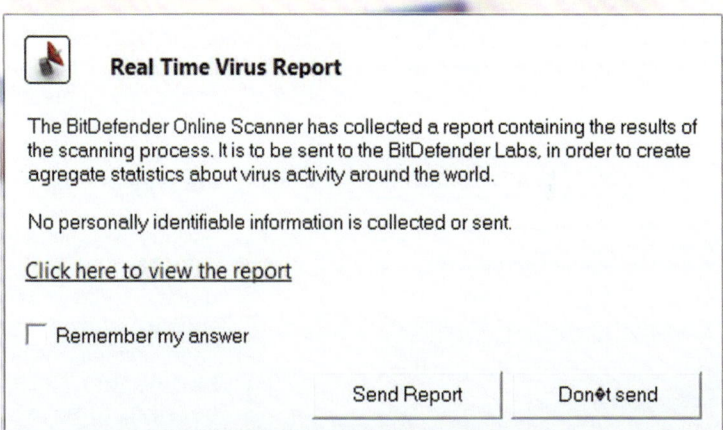

Fig.2.26 The program asks for permission to send a report to the
         BitDefender laboratories

and delete the suspicious files, but it is definitely not a good idea to do so. Decompressing an infected archive can trigger an attack, and the only safe option is to delete the infected archive files.

Bear in mind that deleting files in the normal way will probably just result in them being placed in the Recycle Bin. In other words, they remain on the hard disc drive and the computer remains infected until the offending files are deleted from Recycle Bin. In order to completely remove files it is just a matter of holding down the Shift key while deleting them in the normal way. Alternatively, delete them normally and then go to the recycle bin and "empty" them from the bin. This second method has the advantage of making sure that the files have definitely been removed from the filing system.

The small pop-up window of Figure 2.26 appears when exiting the BitDefender program. It asks for permission to send a report to the BitDefender laboratories, where information about the spread of viruses and other malicious software is gathered. Most of the companies that produce antivirus software seem to gather information of this type. Whether to let the program send the information is up to the individual, but it seems reasonable to do so, especially when using a free antivirus program.

It can sometimes be useful to save a copy of the scan results, especially when the program has been unable to remove all the infections that were detected. The scan reports the names of the infected files, and their locations, which will often be deep in the computer's filing system. This makes it easy to find them if manual deletion is required. The customer support service of the program's manufacturer might be able to give helpful advice about removing awkward viruses, and there are online forums that can also be helpful with this type of thing. In either case it is unlikely that any help will be provided unless you can supply a copy of the scan results. With BitDefender it is possible to save a copy of the scan results in HTML format (Figure 2.27) by operating the "Click here to export the scan report" link when the scan results are displayed (see Figure 2.25). Operating this link produces the usual file browser, and the report can then be saved in the normal way.

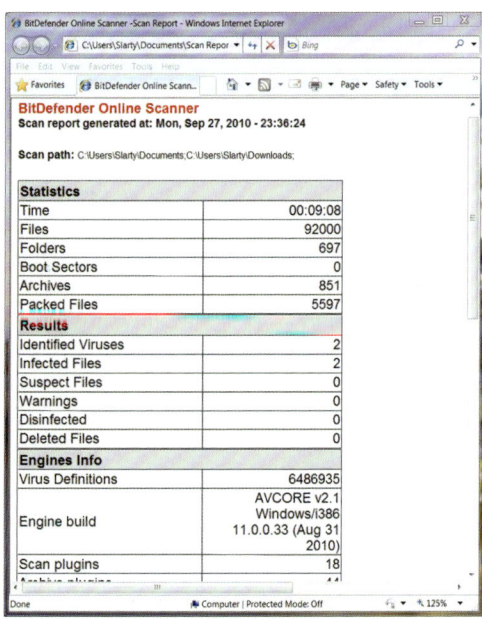

Fig.2.27 The scan report can be saved in HTML format

Malwarebytes

Online scanners are undoubtedly very useful, but having a virus scanner installed on your PC is probably a better way of handling things. If you suspect that your computer has been infected, a built-in virus scanner can be used to immediately check the system for malware. Online scanners are still useful, because they can provide second and third opinions if the built-in scanner fails to find anything. The Malwarebytes virus scanner is a well respected program that is available in free and commercial versions. The full commercial product must be purchased

Fig.2.28 The Malwarebytes home page has a Download button

if real-time protection is required, but the free version is sufficient if on-demand virus scanning is all that is required. The Malwarebytes scanner will operate quite happily while real-time antivirus software is operating, so it is not necessary to switch off any real-time virus protection in order to use this program.

There is a Download button on the Malwarebytes homepage (Figure 2.28), which is at this address:

www.malwarebytes.org

Operating the Download button changes the page to look like Figure 2.29. The program file is not actually downloaded from the Malwarebytes site, and you are instead taken to the relevant section of the CNET.com site. CNET.com is one of the largest sites for downloading free software of various types, and it represents a safe source that should be free of any form of malware. In order to download the program file it is just a matter of operating the Download Now button, and the downloaded file is then run. It will install the program in the normal way.

The screen of Figure 2.30 appears when the program is launched, and the radio buttons provide the option of full or quick scans. As always

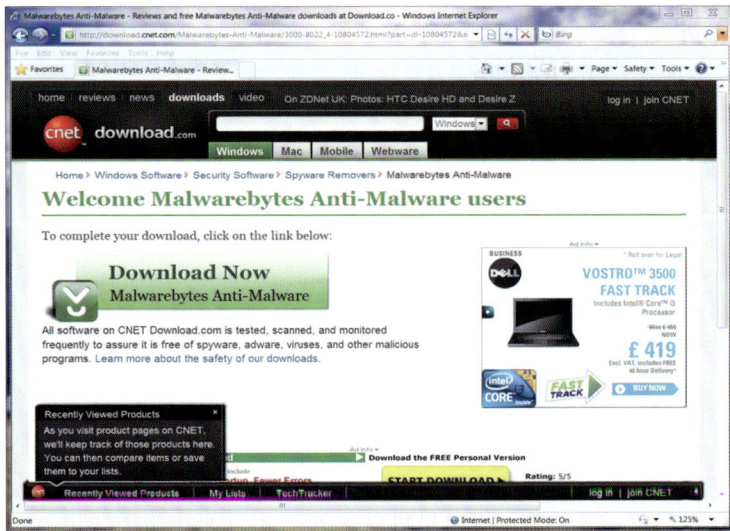

Fig.2.29 The program file is downloaded from the CNET.com site

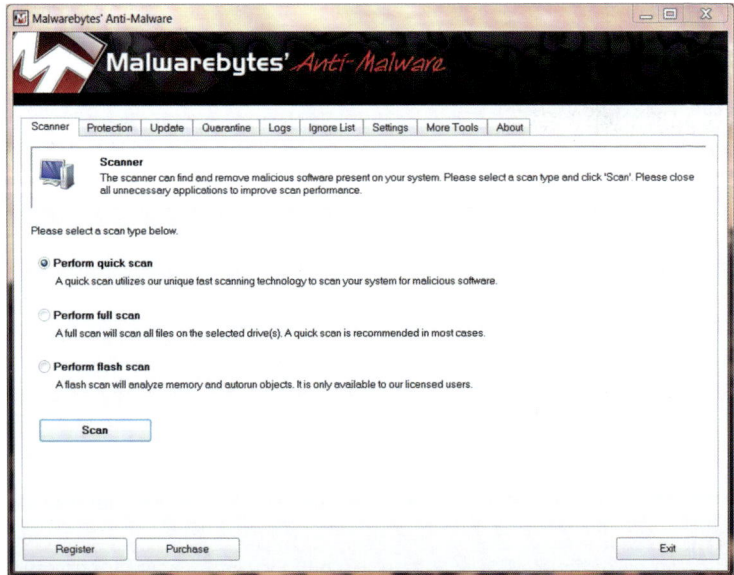

Fig.2.30 The initial screen when the program is launched

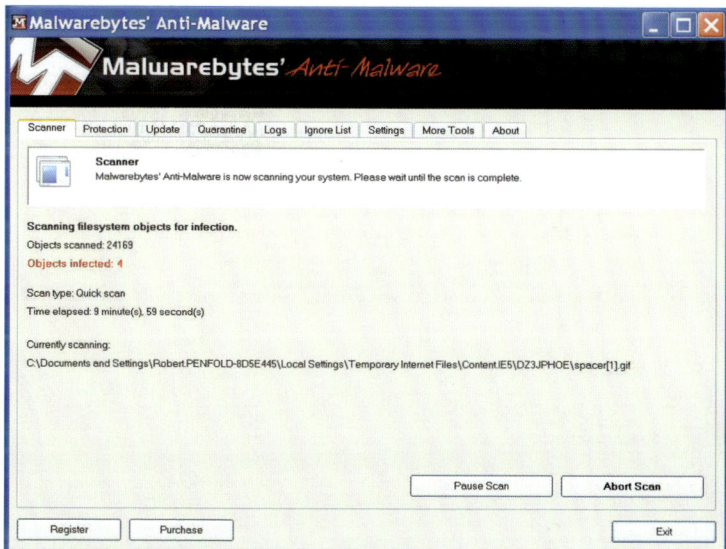

Fig.2.31 The scanning process has started

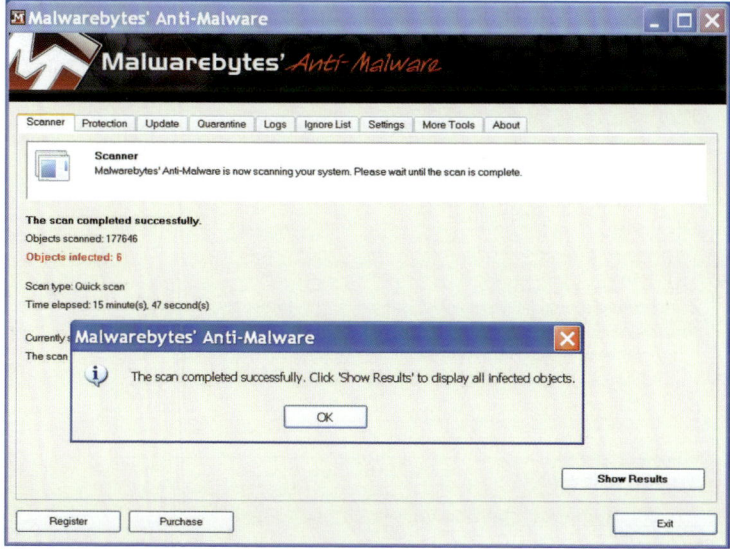

Fig.2.32 The scan has been completed

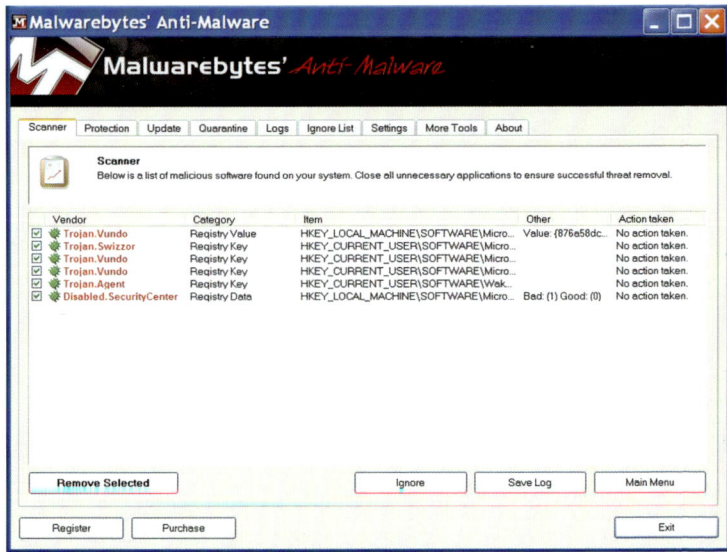

Fig.2.33 The summary of the scan results

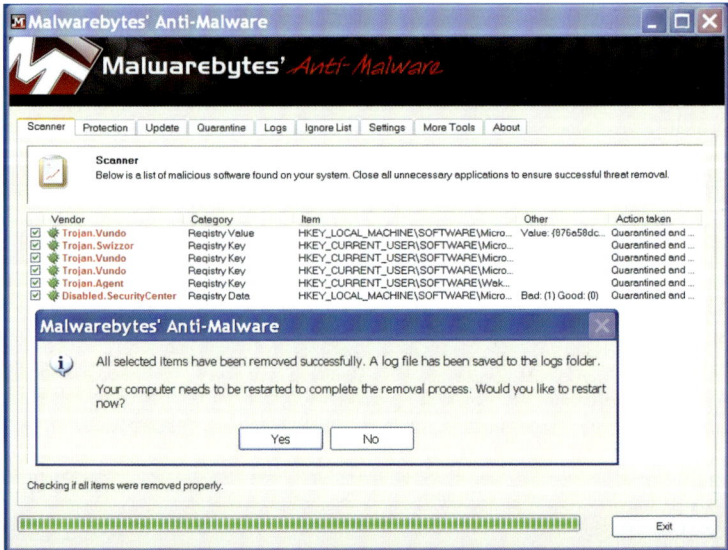

Fig.2.34 The offending items have all been removed

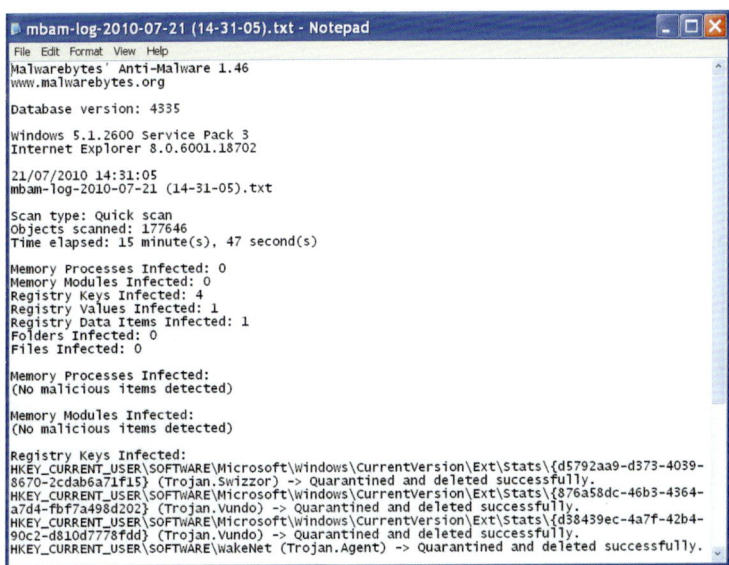

Fig.2.35 A log file can be save to a file

with this type of thing, a full scan can take quite a long time, but a quick scan does not check the entire computer and is not totally reliable. Note that there is a third radio button that provides a flash scan, but this facility is not available in the free version of the program. Operating the Scan button sets things under way with the required type of scan being performed, and the program reports its progress (Figure 2.31).

Eventually the scan will be completed (Figure 2.32), and operating the Show Results button then produces a summary of the results (Figure 2.33). Malwarebytes is not just a scanner, and detected items can be deleted by ticking their checkboxes and operating the Remove Selected button. The program will then report its success or lack of it, as appropriate (Figure 2.34), and it will save a log file (Figure 2.35) on the hard disc drive. It will usually be necessary to restart the computer in order to complete the removal of the malware, and it is advisable to operate the Yes button and restart the computer immediately.

Real-time programs

As pointed out previously, with computer viruses it is a matter of "prevention is better than cure", and the most effective form of protection

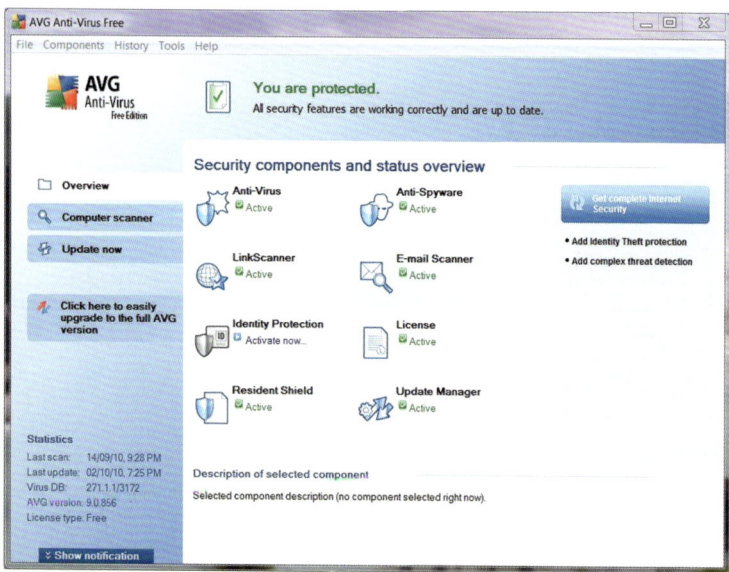

Fig.2.36 The initial screen of AVG Free

is an antivirus program running on your PC that provides real-time protection. In other words, it monitors disc drive activity, Internet activity, or anything that might involve a virus or other malicious program. If any suspicious files are detected, there is an attempt to alter system files, or any dubious activity is detected, the user is warned. In most cases the virus or other malicious program is blocked or removed from the system before it has a chance to do any harm.

There are actually several totally free antivirus programs of this type available as downloads on the Internet. These are genuinely free programs where you do not have to pay any initial fee, or pay a subscription in order to obtain online updates to the virus database. In general, the reputations of these programs are very good, and for home and small business users they genuinely represent a viable alternative to the commercial antivirus suites. The most popular free antivirus software is almost certainly AVG Free from Grisoft, and it is certainly a program that is worth trying. It is the one that will be used here as an example of free real-time antivirus software. The Grisoft site is at:

www.grisoft.com

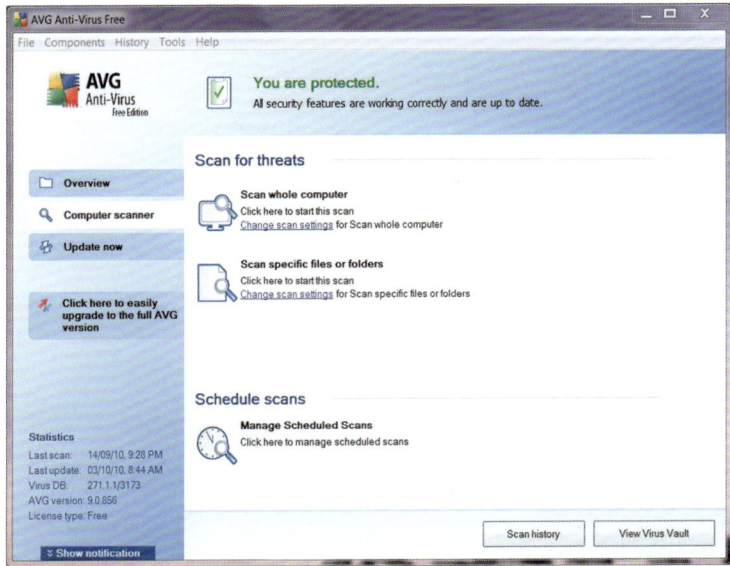

Fig.2.37 The scanner section of the program

On the home page there might be a link to the free version of the program, but it does not seem to feature quite as prominently in the home page as it did in the past. At the time of writing this, the web address for Grisoft's free software is:

http://free.avg.com/download-avg-anti-virus-free-edition

There is an instruction manual for the program in PDF format, and it is possible to read this online provided your PC has the Adobe Acrobat Reader program installed. However, it is definitely a good idea to download the manual and store it on the hard disc drive so that it is handy for future reference. It is a good idea to at least take a quick look through the manual which, amongst other things, provides installation instructions. However, installation is fairly straightforward and follows along the normal lines for Windows software.

Daily updates to AVG are available without a subscription or any other form of payment being required. Although the program is free, it should always be reasonably up-to-date, and it would be a mistake to regard it second best to commercial alternatives. This program has a reputation for being very efficient, and it did once detect a couple of backdoor Trojan

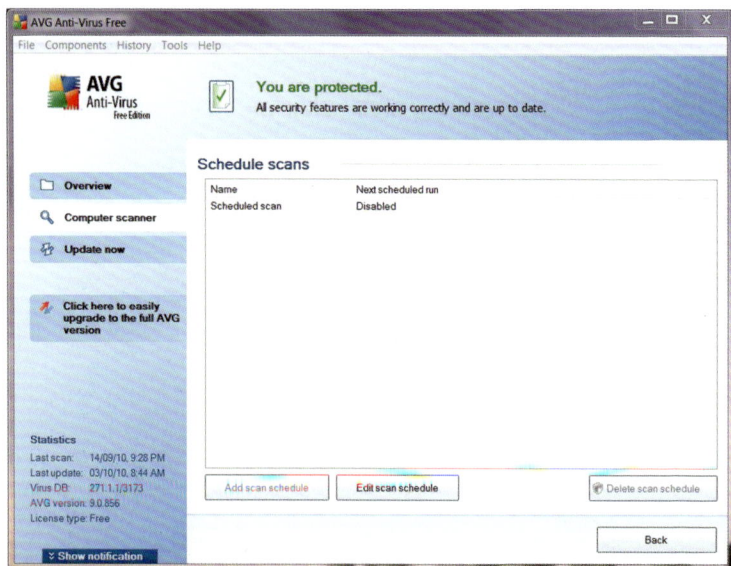

Fig.2.38 This page provides details of any scheduled scans

programs on my system that a certain well known commercial program had failed to detect. It is certainly one of the best freebies on the Internet, and it generally performs very well in comparison to commercial equivalents.

AVG has a useful range of facilities and it is a very capable program. It runs in the background and provides real-time protection, but you can also go into the main program and use some of its facilities manually. It can be launched via the normal routes, and by default there will be a quick-launch button on the taskbar at the bottom of the Windows desktop. The program has various sections, and the initial window provides access to them (Figure 2.36). There is a facility here that manually updates the program's virus database, but the program will automatically update provided an active Internet link is available when the program is booted into Windows.

In common with most antivirus programs you can set it to scan the system on a regular basis. First operate the Computer scanner tab in the left-hand section of the window, and then operate the Schedule scans link when the window changes to look like Figure 2.37. Any scheduled scans will then be shown, and in this example (Figure 2.38) there are none

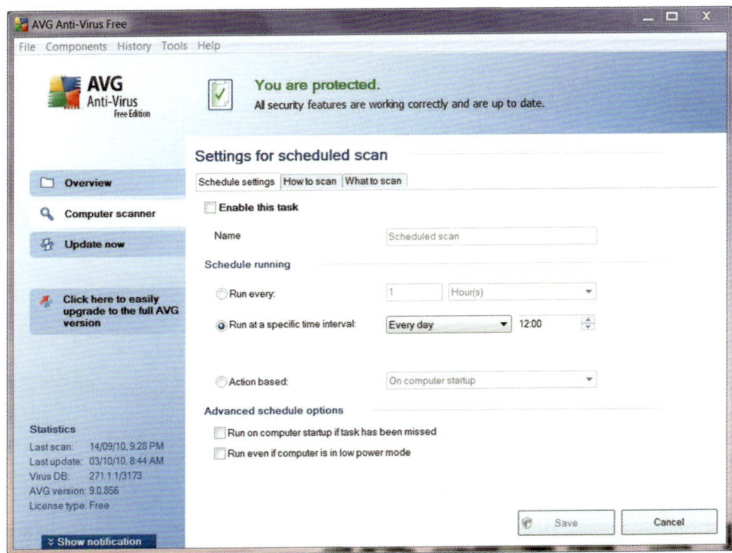

Fig.2.39 This page can be used to set up a scanning schedule

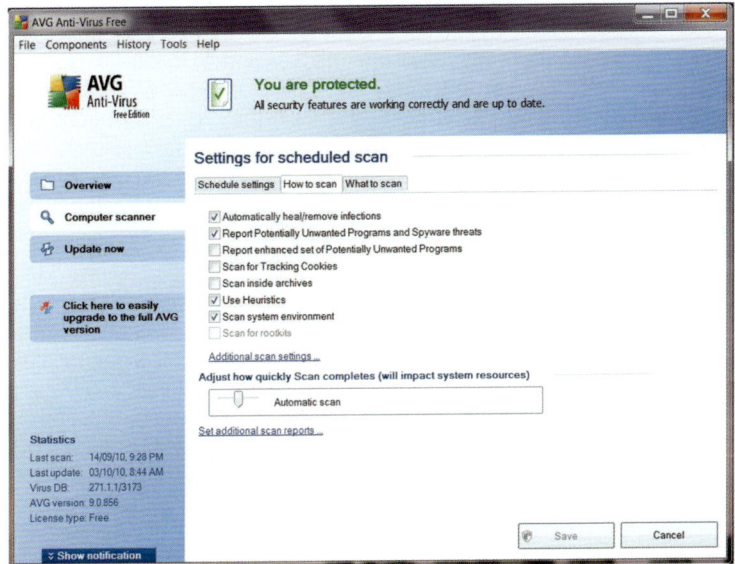

Fig.2.40 This page enables the type of scanning to be altered

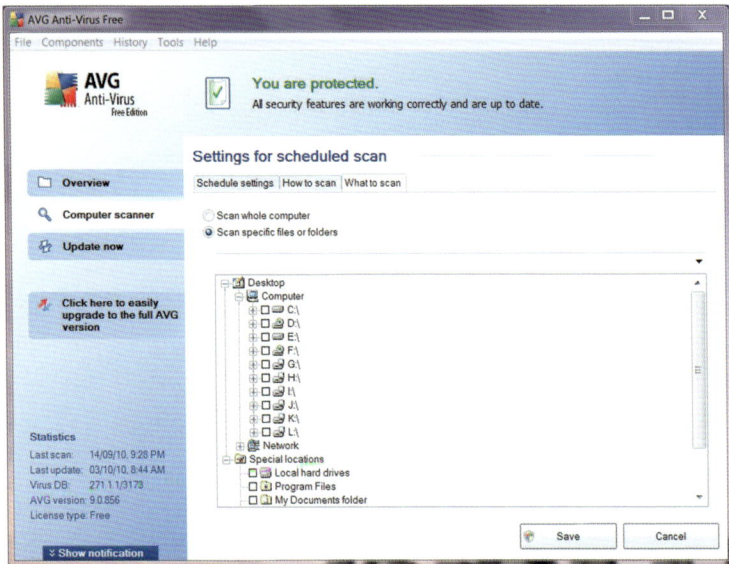

Fig.2.41 It is possible to scan only selected parts of the system

listed. In order to set up regular scanning, start by operating the "Edit
scan schedule" button, which will change the window to look like Figure
2.39. The checkbox near the top of the window must be ticked in order
to switch on scheduled scanning, and then the required options are
selected. The available timing options in the free version of AVG are
sparser than those in the full version, but they should still be perfectly
adequate for most purposes. The additional two tabs near the top of the
window provide access to the type of scanning used (Figure 2.40) and
the parts of the system that are scanned (Figure 2.41).

A scan can be started manually by selecting the appropriate link in the
upper part of the scanning window (Figure 2.37). This provides options
for scanning the entire computer or selected areas. Choosing the latter
produces a window that is essentially the same as the one of Figure
2.41, and the required areas are then selected by ticking the appropriate
checkboxes. You can use this method to scan a single file or folder, but
it is usually quicker and easier to do this by locating the file or folder
using Windows Explorer. Select the file or folder and then right-click it
(Figure 2.42). This produces a pop-up menu where the "Scan with AVG
Free" option is selected. As usual, the program will report the progress

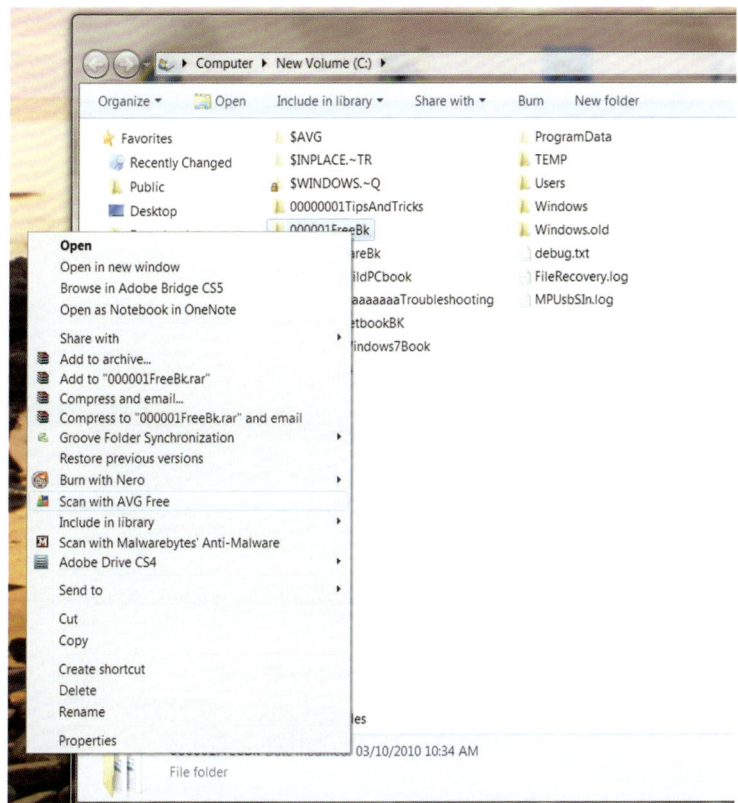

Fig.2.42 It is easy to scan just a single file or folder

made while a scan is running (Figure 2.43), and a full set of results is provide once the scan has been completed (Figure 2.44). In this case nothing suspicious was found.

AVG Free is not just a scanner, and it will try to remove any infections that are found. It is only fair to point out again that an antivirus program can not automatically remove every type of computer infection. Most can be dealt with automatically, but some have to be removed manually. In such cases the program will usually provide removal instructions, or take you to a web site where detailed instructions can be found. Some of the steps required can be a bit technical, but everything should be fine provided you follow the instructions "to the letter". However, if you

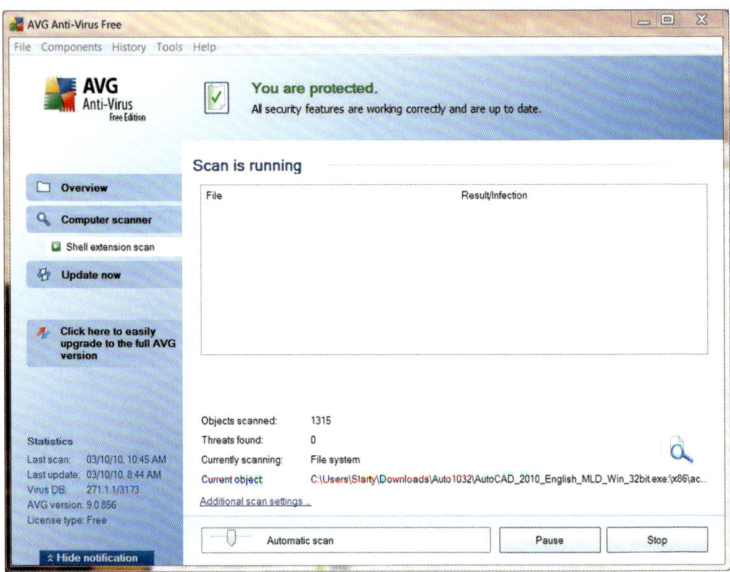

Fig.2.43 The program reports its progress during a scan

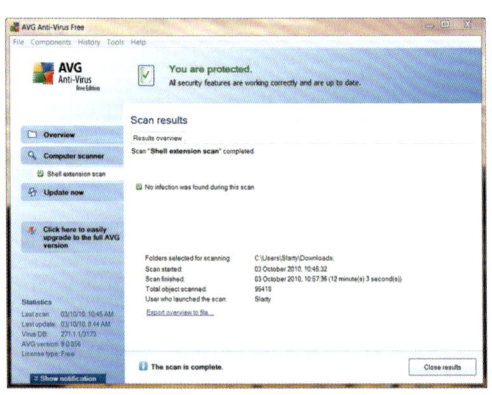

have a friend or relative who has a fair amount of computing expertise, enlisting their help is probably a good idea, for peace of mind if nothing else.

Fig.2.44 The scan is complete and the results are displayed

Other security software

More the merrier

Modern antivirus programs tend to provide more than virus scanning and real-time antivirus protection. Even the free version of the AVG does rather more than this, with a link scanner, Email scanner, and an anti-spyware program in addition to the antivirus program. Windows itself has a built-in anti-spyware program and a basic firewall. This has reduced the need for additional security software, but it has not totally removed it. It might be necessary to use an additional program to fill a gap left by the

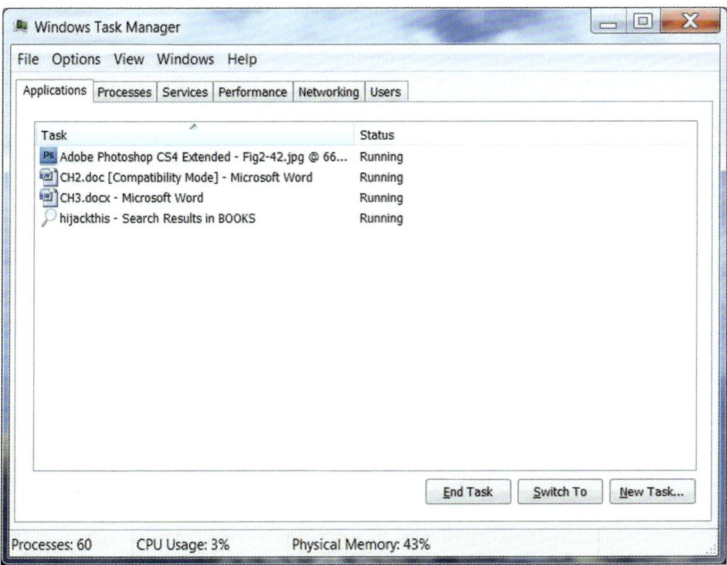

Fig.3.1 Task Manager showing the running applications

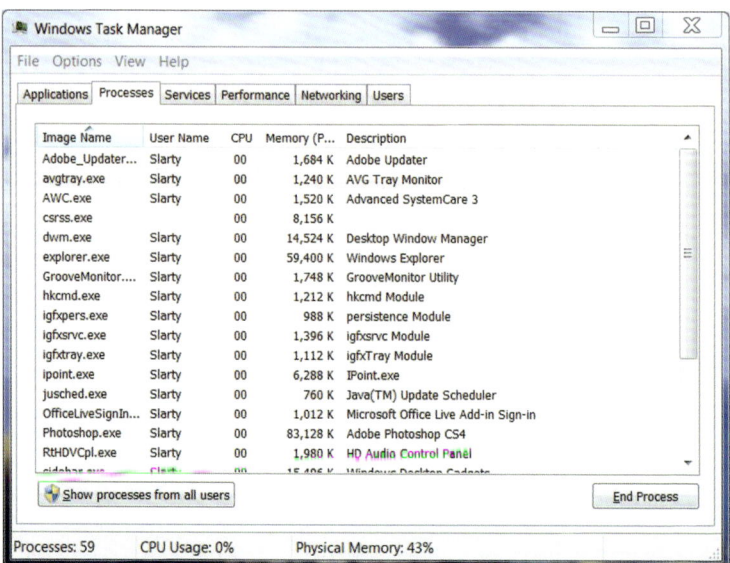

*Fig.3.2 There will probably be numerous entries under the Processes
tab*

particular security software you are using, or you might be dissatisfied
with an aspect of it, and would like to try an alternative.

If you feel that there is a problem and that the security software you have
tried is not getting to the heart of the problem, then it might be worth
trying security software that adopts a different approach to things. Using
several different approaches increases the chances of finding and
defeating any malware that has infected your computer. With an awkward
infection the "more the merrier" approach will usually cure the problem.

Task Manager

When you suspect that malware is present on your PC, but it is somehow
managing to evade detection, a useful next step is to investigate the
running applications and processes using the Windows Task Manager.
With Windows 7 the Task Manager can be launched using the Control –
Shift – Escape key combination. By default it will show the application

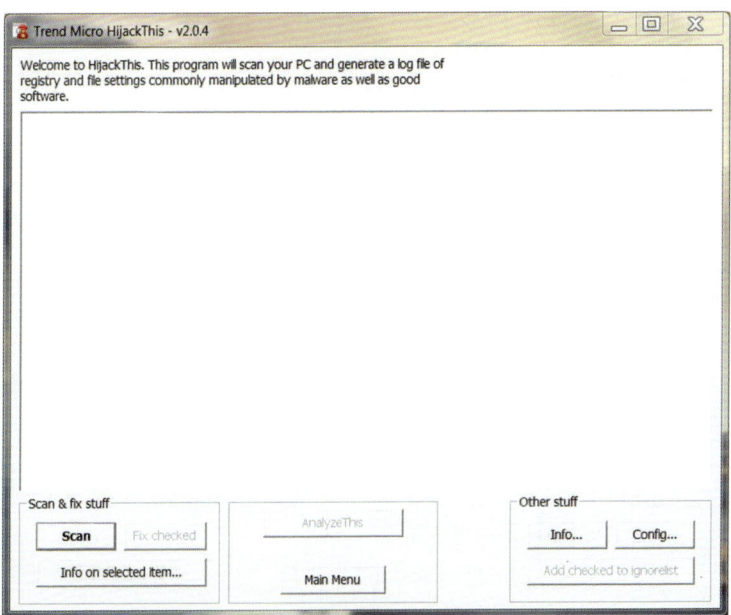

Fig.3.3 The initial screen of HijackThis

software that is being run by the current user (Figure 3.1), but a list of the background processes can be obtained by operating the Processes tab (Figure 3.2).

Once Task Manager is running you can look for any programs or processes that should not be there. If you are not sure about any of them it is easy to find details using a search engine such as Google. Use the name of the process plus the word "process" as the search string, and several links to sites giving basic details of it should be found. Try to avoid jumping to conclusions with this type of thing.

There will usually be a large number of processes, and many of them will probably have unfamiliar names. Most will be legitimate processes though, and will either be part of the Windows operating system or associated with application programs installed on your computer. It is therefore essential to check that suspect processes are indeed dodgy, and not part of software that you use. Note that there will often be running processes that are part of application programs that are not actually running on your computer at the time.

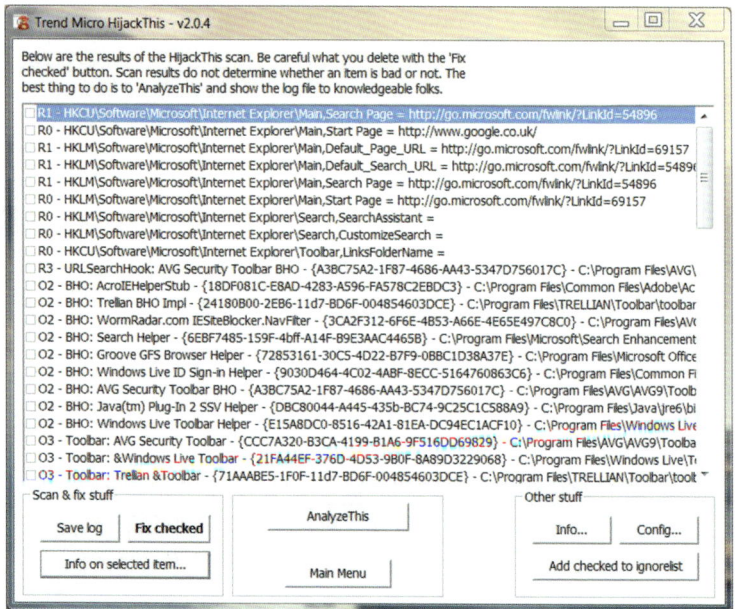

Fig.3.4   The list of results. Most of the changes and processes listed will be legitimate

HijackThis

A program called HijackThis (Figure 3.3) is available as a free download from the usual sources such as CNET.com and download.com, and this can be used to show a list of changes to the system and suspicious processes (Figure 3.4). The program will try to undo changes if the checkboxes for the relevant entries are ticked and the "Fix checked" button is operated. Again, be aware that most of the things it lists will be perfectly legitimate processes and changes. For example, if you add a toolbar to Internet Explorer or do practically any customisation, the changes will be included in the HijackThis report.

In order to use a program such as this you need a fair amount of expertise, or must obtain specialist help from one of the web sites that offer assistance in dealing with computer infections. More information on a suspect entry can be obtained by selecting it and operating the "Info on selected item" button (Figure 3.5). If you decide to seek expert advice, operating the AnalyzeThis button launches the default browser and takes

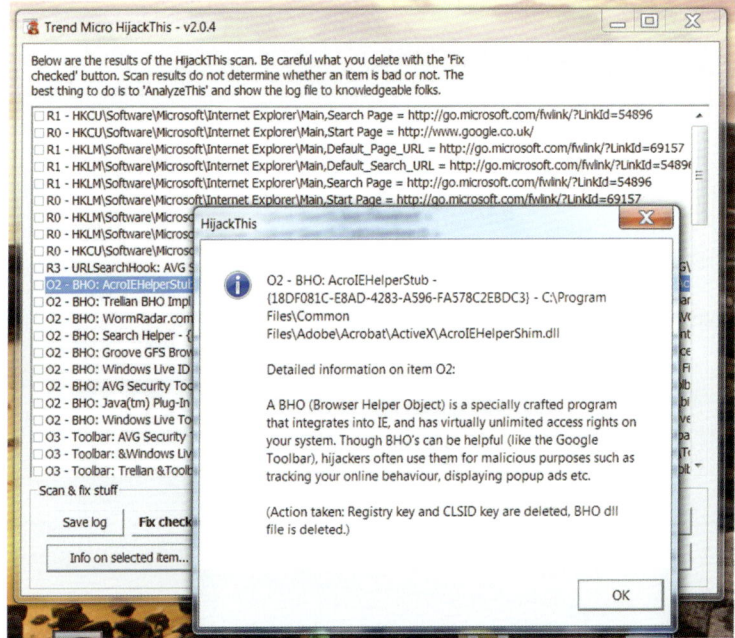

Fig.3.5 Further information is available for each item

you to a page that links to HijackThis forums in various languages (Figure 3.6).

Recurring problems

Having found a malicious program by whatever means, you can use the normal search facilities of Windows Explorer to locate and delete the offending program file. Do not be surprised if the offending program simply reappears the next time the computer is booted into Windows. This can also occur when using an antimalware program to remove infections. Many modern computer pests are designed so that a file is installed and run each time the computer is booted into the operating system. Hence the deleted program runs again when the computer is rebooted. It is the source of the offending file that is the real problem.

This problem is less likely to occur when using an antimalware program to remove the infection, because the program will usually be designed

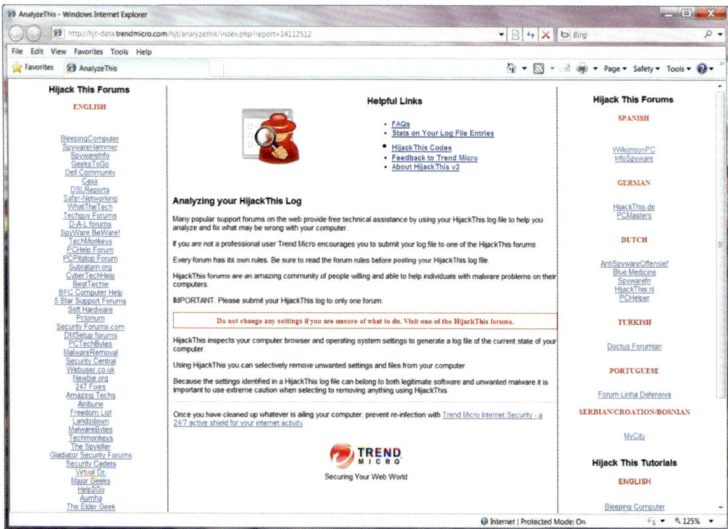

Fig.3.6 Help is available from forums in various languages

to get to the root of the problem and eliminate its source. However, there is no guarantee that this will always be the case. With the more difficult infections an Internet search will usually provide details for completely removing the malware, but the process is not always entirely straightforward. If you lack the necessary expertise it is a good idea to seek the help of a friend or family member who is good at this type of thing.

Changing times

At one time it was normal to use separate programs for handling the various types of computer infection. This was in the days when the vast majority of infections were viruses, and other types such as Trojans and spyware were relatively rare. This state of affairs was transposed over a period of time, and it is now the viruses that are in the minority, and infections such as Trojans and spyware that are the main problem. Most estimates suggest that viruses only account for about two or three percent of computer infections. The popular antivirus programs have had to be adapted to encompass this change, and they now detect and deal with most types of computer infection.

Fig.3.7 The initial screen of the Ad-Aware program

The need for specialist programs for detecting and removing Trojans, adware, and spyware has reduced, but some computer users still prefer to use what they perceive to be "the right tool for the job". Specialist antimalware programs can also be useful when used in addition to normal antivirus programs, and are especially useful when you suspect that your computer is infected, but antivirus software has failed to find anything.

Spyware/adware detection

A program called Ad-Aware has for many years been the most popular program for detecting and removing adware and spyware. In the same way that normal antivirus programs have expanded their repertoire to match changing circumstances, programs such as Ad-Aware have also changed to encompass a greater range of threats. The latest version of Ad-Aware includes a limited degree of real-time protection, but it remains primarily a scanner for combating adware and spyware. It remains one of the best programs available for dealing with these types of computer infection.

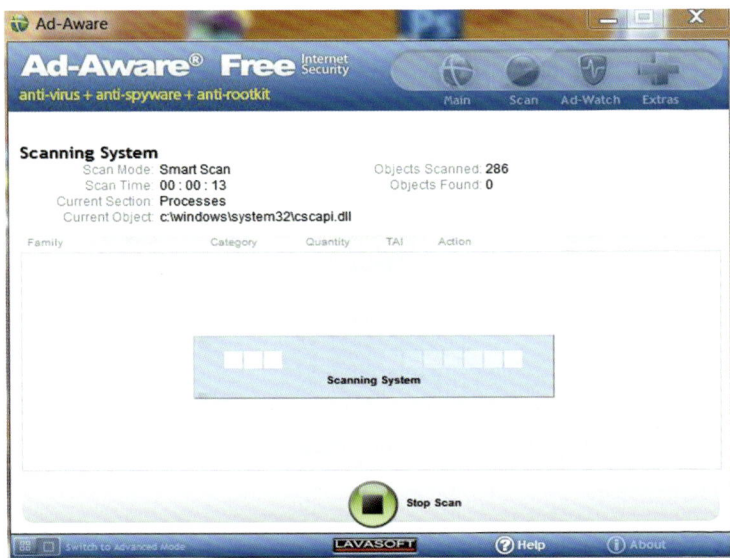

Fig.3.8 A status screen shows how the scan is progressing

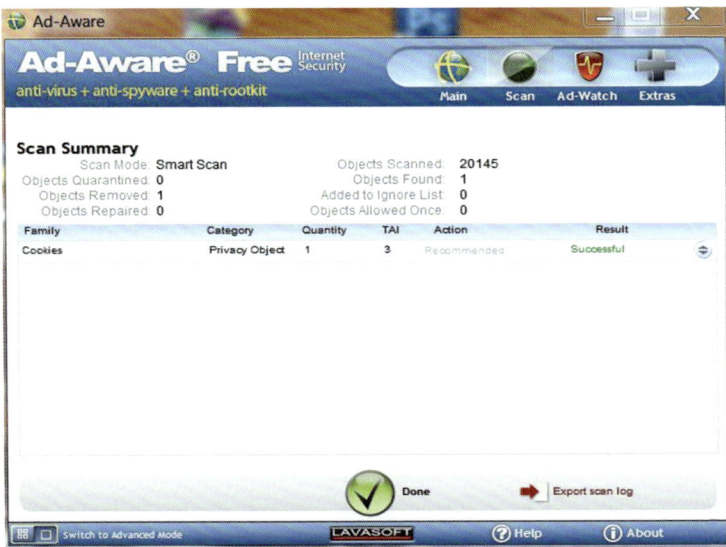

Fig.3.9 A list of results and the actions taken is provided

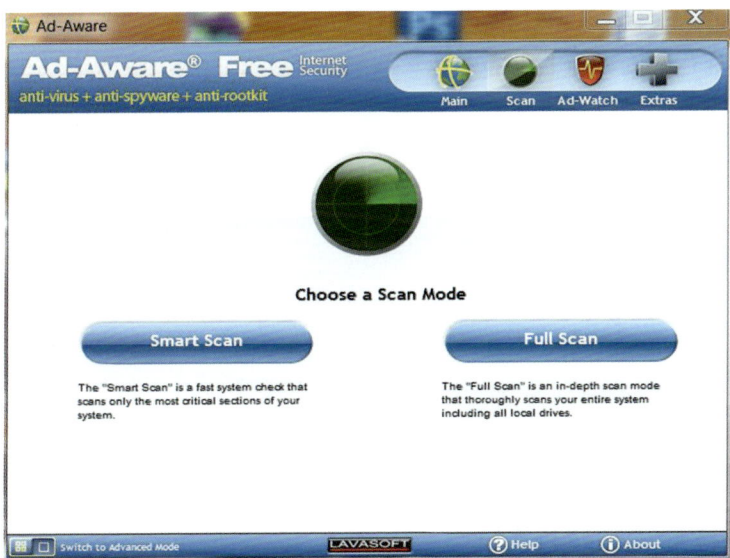

Fig.3.10 A full scan option is available

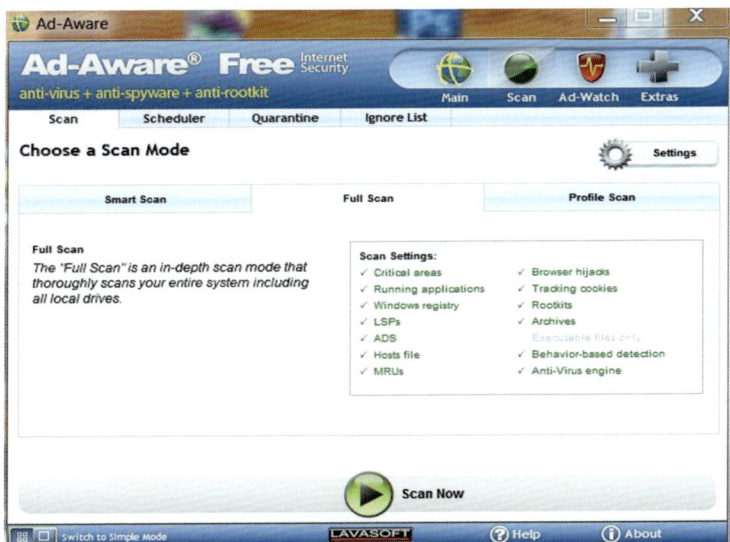

Fig.3.11 More options are available if Advanced mode is selected

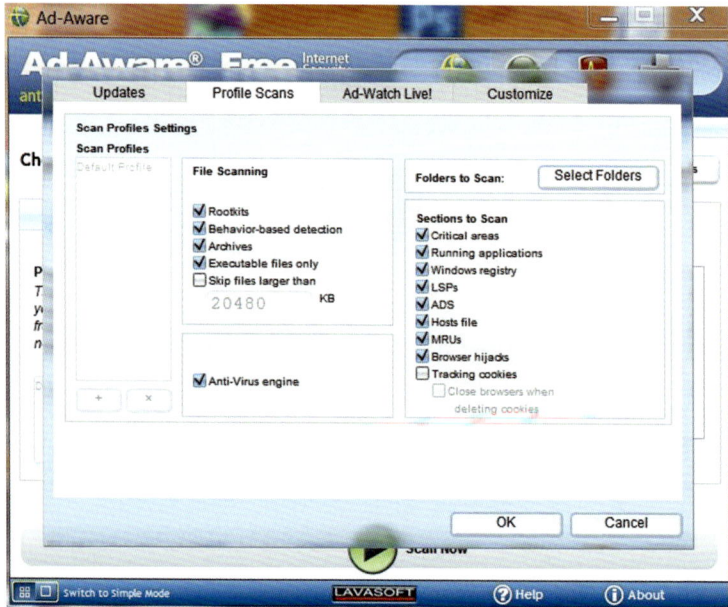

Fig.3.12 A custom scanning mode can be set up

Ad-Aware is available from the usual sources of free software, and from the web site of its writers (www.lavasoft.com). It used to be quite a small download, but with the current version, and once the updates have been downloaded as well, it could total well in excess of 200 megabytes. This is just about possible with an ordinary dial-up Internet connection of good quality, but some form of broadband connection is clearly preferable for this type of thing.

The main window of Figure 3.7 is obtained when Ad-Aware is run for the first time. If the program was not updated as part of the installation process it is important to operate the Web Update button and update the database before proceeding further. With the program up-to-date, a scan can be started manually by operating the Scan System button. A status screen will then appear (Figure 3.8), and this will show how the scan is progressing. The Smart Scan feature will be used by default, and this only scans the parts of the system where problems are most likely to be found. A report showing the threats found and the actions taken (Figure 3.9) will be shown once the scan has been completed.

Fig.3.13 Select the Freeware mode

A more in-depth scan can be obtained by operating the Scan button near the top of the main window, and then selecting Full Scan (Figure 3.10). The program goes into Simple mode by default, but using the two buttons in the bottom left-hand corner of the window it is possible to switch between Simple mode and Advanced mode (Figure 3.11). The Advanced mode gives more control over the way scans operate, and it is possible to set up your own custom scanning mode (Figure 3.12). However, for most purposes the Smart Scan and Full Scan modes should suffice.

Trojan removers

There are a number of programs that are primarily aimed at removing Trojans, but as with other antimalware programs, these have mostly developed into programs that provide more than Trojan scanning and removal. Some users still prefer these programs when the suspected threat is some form of Trojan, and Emsisoft Antimalware is one of the more highly regarded free programs for combating Trojans. It can be obtained from the usual sources of free software.

Fig.3.14 The program must be updated before it can be used

Fig.3.15 The initial screen once into the main program

Fig.3.16 Various scanning options are available

Fig.3.17 As usual, a status screen shows how things are progressing

Fig.3.18 The scan has been completed and no threats were found

When running the program for the first time you have to choose the required version (Figure 3.13), and the Freeware option should be selected. In this mode the program operates as a scanner, with no real-time protection being provided. As usual, the program has to be updated before it is used for the first time (Figure 3.14), and various options are available via the radio buttons. Once into the main program (Figure 3.15) the first task is to run a scan, and you are provided with a choice of several types (Figure 3.16). The Deep Scan option is the one that provides the most detailed scan, and it is the one that should normally be used. An information screen shows how the scan is progressing (Figure 3.17), and the results are displayed once the scanning has been completed (Figure 3.18). No threats were detected in this example.

Firewall

A firewall can be either a piece of hardware or a program running in the background. A firewall's basic function is much the same whether it is implemented in software or hardware. Although some people seem to think that a firewall and antivirus programs are the same, there are major differences. There is often some overlap between real world antivirus

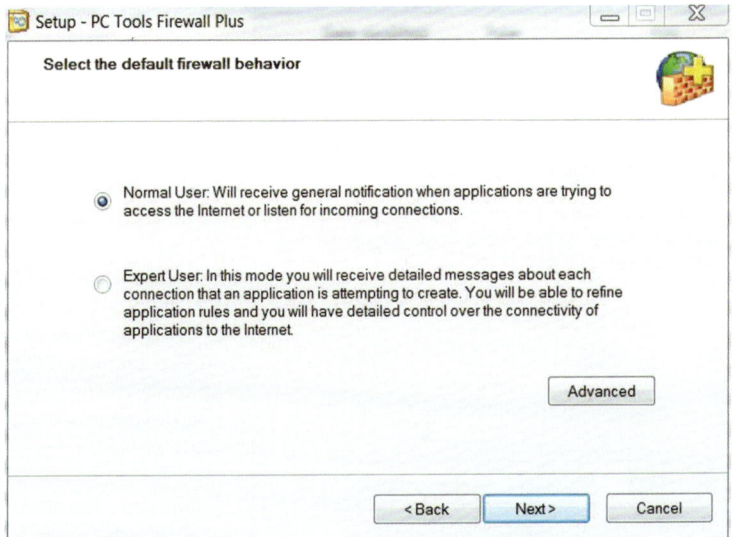

Fig.3.19 There is a choice of Normal and Expert modes

and firewall programs, but their primary aims are different. An antivirus program is designed to scan files on discs and the contents of the computer's memory in search of viruses and other potentially harmful files. Having found any suspect files, the program will usually deal with them. A firewall is used to block access to your PC, and in most cases it is access to your PC via the Internet that is blocked. Bear in mind though, that a software firewall will usually block access via a local area network (LAN) as well.

Of course, a firewall is of no practical value if it blocks communication from one PC to another and access via the Internet. What it is actually doing is preventing unauthorised access to the protected PC. When you access an Internet site your PC sends messages to the server hosting that site, and these messages request the pages you wish to view. Having requested information, the PC expects information to be sent from the appropriate server, and it accepts that information when it is received. A firewall does not interfere with this type of Internet activity provided it is set up correctly.

It is a different matter when another system tries to access your PC when you have not instigated the initial contact. The firewall will treat this

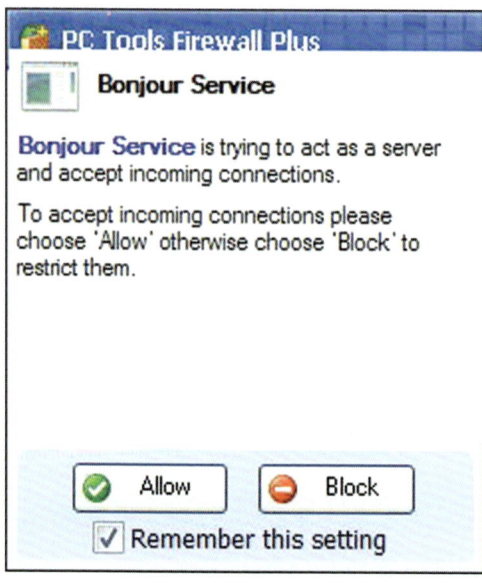

Fig.3.20 A program is trying to use the Internet

attempted entry as an attack and will block it. Of course, the attempt at accessing your PC might not be an attack, and a firewall can result in legitimate access being blocked. Something like P2P file swapping is likely to fail or operate in a limited fashion. The sharing of files and resources on a local area network could also be blocked. A practical firewall enables the user to permit certain types of access so that the computer can work normally while most unauthorised access is still blocked. However, doing so does reduce the degree of protection provided by the firewall.

Although a firewall is primarily intended to prevent hackers from gaining access to your PC via the Internet, it is also designed to provide protection in the opposite direction. In other words, it will prevent programs running on the computer from gaining unauthorised access to the Internet. This is important aspect of a firewall, because some types of malware, such as backdoor Trojans, are designed to gather personal information and then send it to hackers via the Internet. A firewall should inform you if a piece of malware tries to access the Internet, and it should also enable the malware to be blocked.

PC Tools Firewall Plus

Modern versions of Windows include a basic firewall as standard, and many broadband routers include this facility. Consequently, additional firewall protection will not always be needed. It is still worth considering if you use some form of dial-up Internet connection, especially if it is a

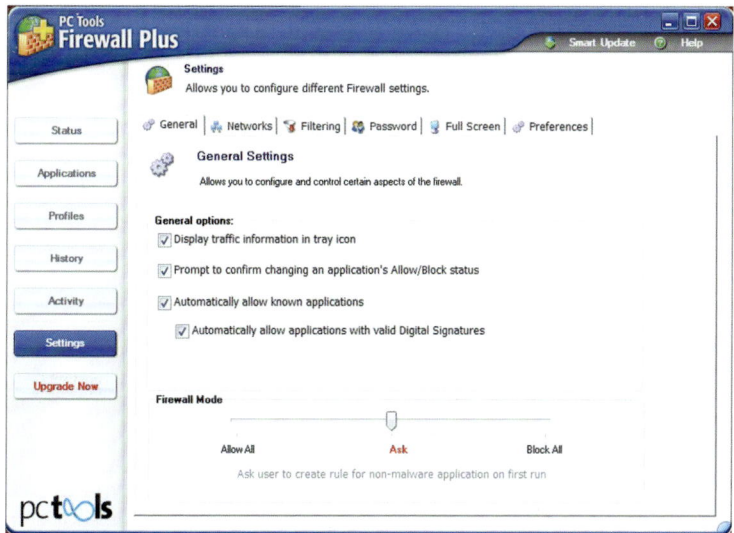

Fig.3.21 Adjustments can be made via the Settings tab

broadband type such as a mobile broadband connection. There are several good free firewall programs available from the usual sources of free downloads, and the one that will be used as the basis of this example is PC Tools Firewall Plus.

When the program is run for the first time you are given a choice of using Normal and Expert modes (Figure 3.19). The program actually operates in much the same way in both modes, and the main difference is the amount of detail provided when the program reports that an application is trying to access the Internet. The Normal mode should provide sufficient information for most users.

In use the program runs in the background and remains largely unseen. However, it will provide an onscreen message (Figure 3.20) when a potentially suspicious program tries to access the Internet for the first time. In most cases it will be obvious that the reported program is one that is completely legitimate, but there could be programs that are not obviously part of your normal online activity. In this example the Bonjour Service was not an application program that I was running on the computer, and it was not obviously part of an application program such as an automatic update service.

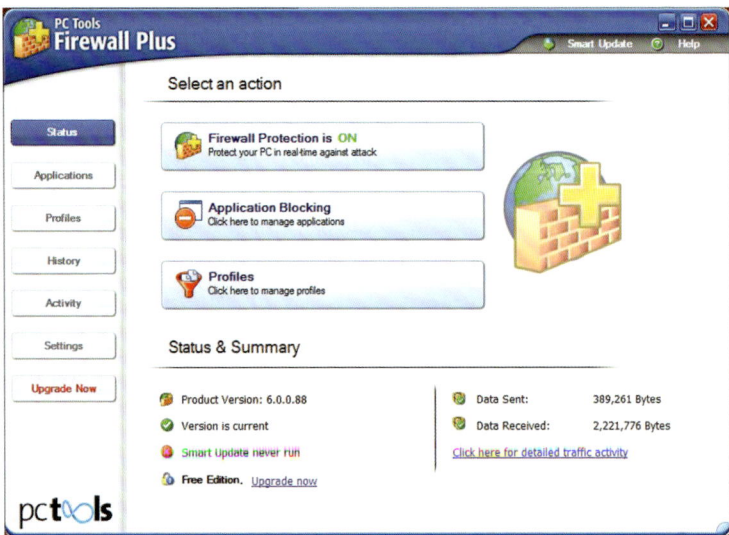

Fig.3.22 General information is available via the Status tab

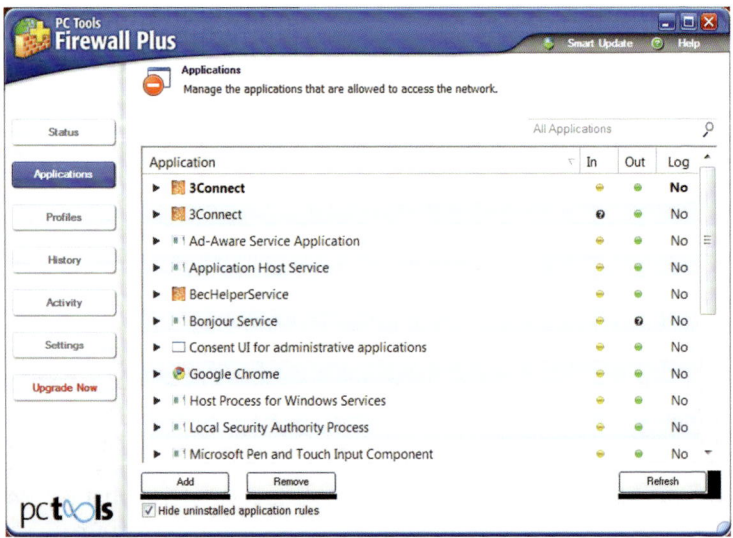

Fig.3.23 You can check the type of access available to each program

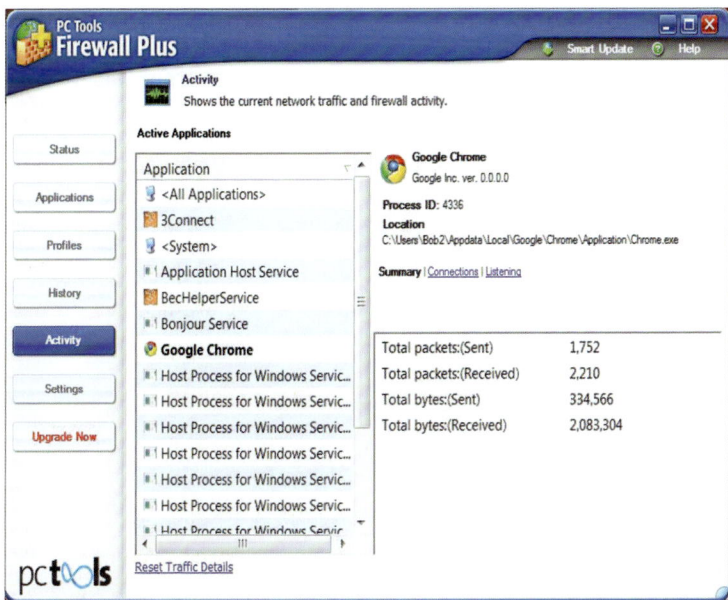

Fig.3.24 The Activity tab provides a log of Internet accesses

Some investigation on the Internet revealed that it is part of the Apple iTunes program, but this software was not installed on this particular PC. Further investigations revealed that the Bonjour Service was also part of certain Adobe applications, and this was the reason for it being run on the test PC. It was therefore safe to allow it to access the Internet. If in doubt though, always block suspicious services from the Internet.

Although it normally operates in the background, it is possible to launch the program and then make adjustments to the way it works via the Settings tab (Figure 3.21). The Status tab (Figure 3.22) can be used to obtain general information about the operation of the program. Using the Applications tab (Figure 3.23) you can check the type of access, if any, allowed for various programs. It is also possible to make changes here, which is important. Should you block access for a program and then find that an important facility no longer operates as a result, you can use this section of the firewall program to reinstate Internet access for the blocked facility. The Activity tab (Figure 3.24) provides a log of recent activity so you can check which programs have accessed the Internet.

When using a firewall such as PC Tools Firewall Plus there will usually be a fair number of alerts popping up when the program is used for the first few times. It will query any Internet accesses that are anything other than normal Windows activity, and with modern software this tends to produce numerous onscreen messages. However, this excess activity should soon diminish to virtually nothing as you indicate which programs should have Internet access, and those if any, that should be blocked. You are effectively teaching the firewall program a set of rules that it will use in the future each time the computer is run. It is worth taking a little time and effort to get the teaching process right. There is otherwise a risk that you will produce a set of rules that hinder a legitimate process, or that you will tell the firewall to give uninhibited Internet access to a piece of malware!

Tuning
software

Risks

There are numerous utilities that can help to speed up a computer that is starting to slow down, and various tweaks that can be made to the Windows Registry in order to ensure that the computer runs at optimum efficiency. It is only fair to point out that practically any method of tuning a computer for optimum efficiency is likely to involve a certain amount of risk to the operating system. Dabbling with the operating system when you do not have the necessary expertise is a common way of rendering

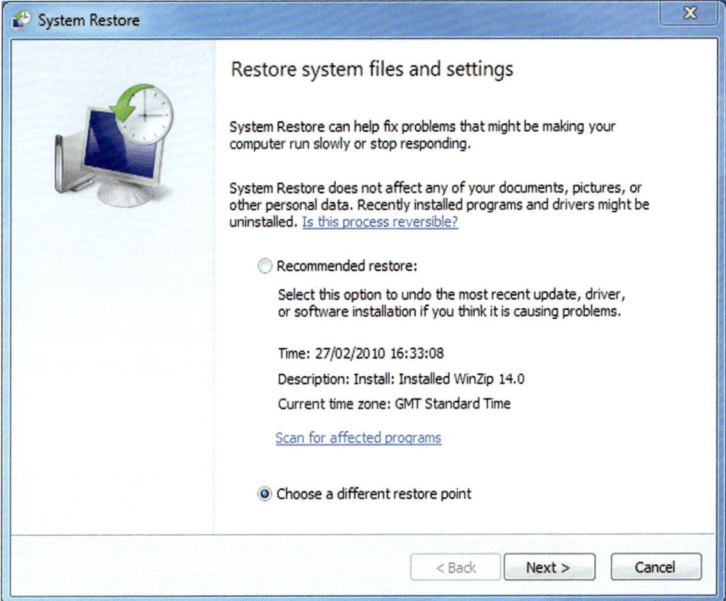

Fig.4.1 The initial screen of System Restore

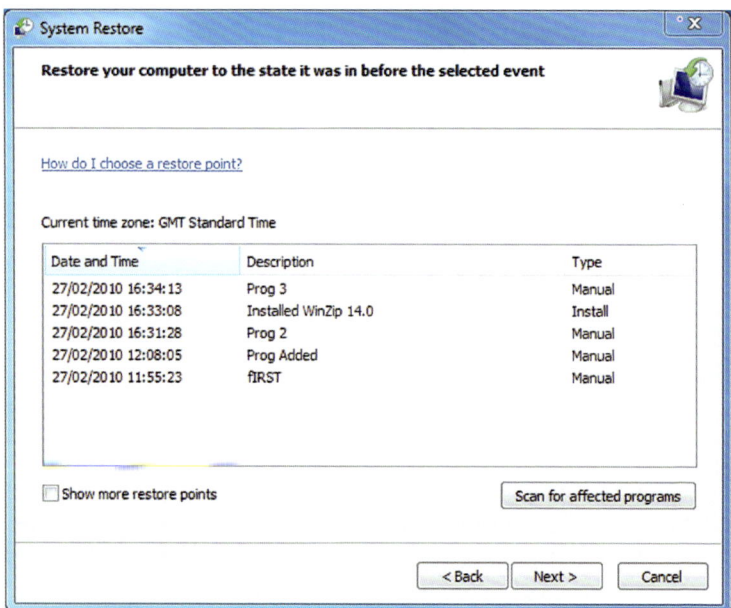

Fig.4.2 You can select any one of the available restoration points

a PC unbootable. Using a good tuning utility to handle the task for you is a much safer way of doing things, but is not completely free of risk.

I am not suggesting that tuning of a PC should always be avoided due to the perils involved, and the risks of damaging the operating system are very low if reputable tuning utilities are used. However, it is a good idea to be prepared for problems just in case anything should go wrong. The ideal approach is to make sure that a complete backup of the hard disc drive is made before any tuning is carried out. The minimum that should be done is to make a restoration point using the Windows System Restore facility prior to using any tuning utility. Many tuning utilities will actually do this as part of the tuning process.

System Restore

This is one of the best repair facilities available when using Windows, and it will often provide a quick and easy solution when the computer has major or minor problems. The idea of System Restore is to take the operating system back to its state at an earlier date when the PC did

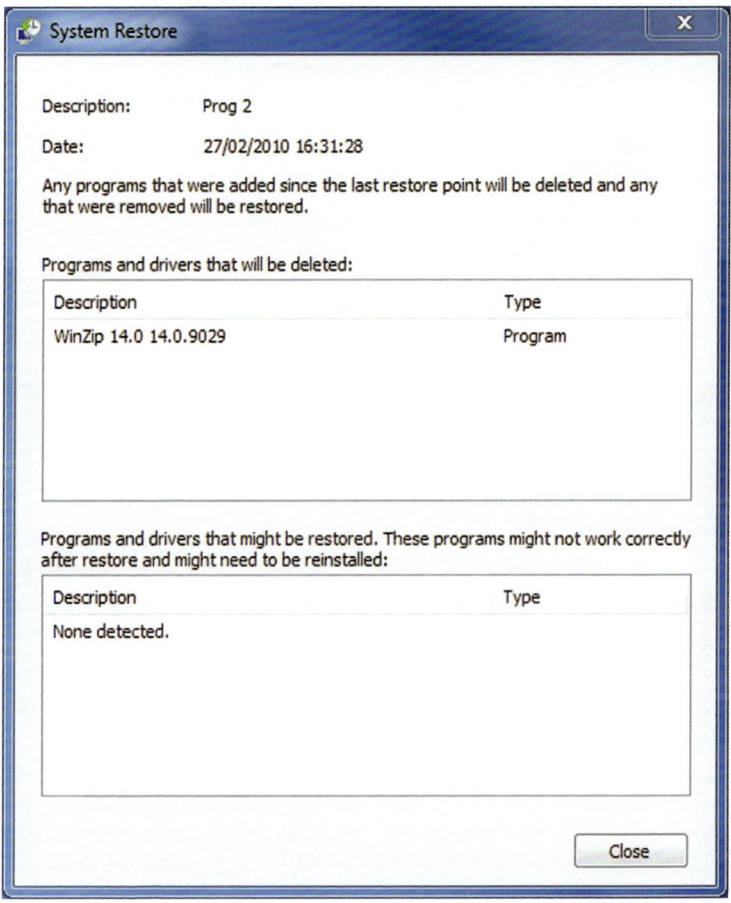

Fig.4.3 You can check to see if any programs will be uninstalled

boot into Windows and function properly. The System Restore facility is available from within Windows, but this is clearly of no use unless the computer can be booted into Windows. However, there are other ways of entering this facility.

For the moment, we will assume that it is possible to boot into Windows and launch the System Restore program. This is achieved by going to the Start menu and choosing All Programs, Accessories, System Tools, and System Restore. There might be a delay of a minute or two while

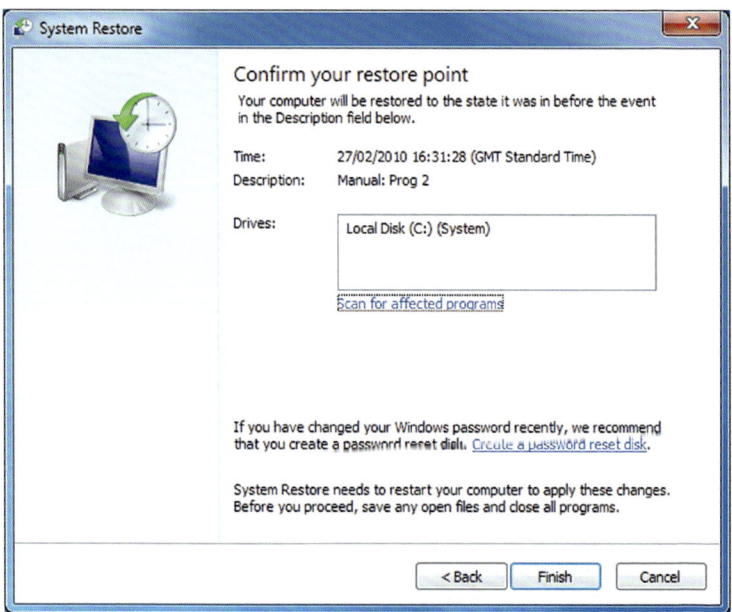

Fig.4.4 You must confirm that the selected settings are correct

the system is scanned, but eventually a window like the one in Figure 4.1 will be launched.

Reverting to a restoration point is reasonably straightforward. In this example a restoration point is being recommended, and this will usually be the latest one that is available. You can opt to use a different one though, and this is the only course of action if the program does not suggest a restoration point. A window like the one of Figure 4.2 will be produced if you elect to choose a restoration point. Using System Restore should not result in any data files being lost, but taking Windows back to an earlier state can result in recently installed programs being uninstalled.

Problems with Windows are sometimes caused by installing a program that does not fully conform to the Windows rules, and its removal could be an essential part of getting the system working properly again. However, in the current context this is unlikely to be relevant. Provided a restoration point was made immediately prior to tuning the system, it will only be the changes made by the tuning program that will be reversed, and it will only be these changes that need to be reversed.

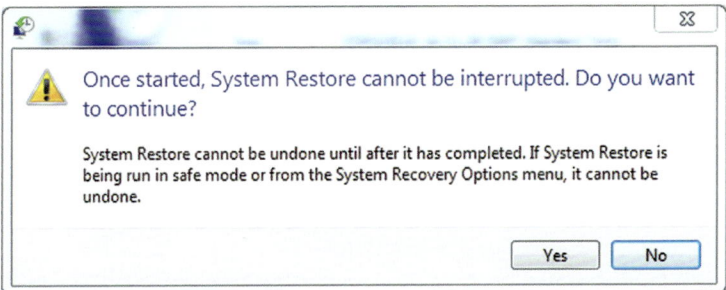

Fig.4.5 Once started, the restoration process must be allowed to finish

If no restoration point was made prior to using the tuning utility, it is possible to check to see if any programs will be affected by a given restoration point. It is just a matter of left-clicking the entry for the appropriate point and operating the "Scan for affected programs" button. There will be a delay while the system is scanned, and then the results will be shown (Figure 4.3). The upper panel shows the programs that will effectively be uninstalled, and the lower panel lists any driver software that will have to be reinstalled. In this example only one program is affected. Of course, you will lose any changes at all made to the Windows settings since the restoration point was made, and not just those made by the tuning utility. This includes things like changes to the Windows desktop and screen settings.

After selecting a restoration point you are asked to confirm that the correct settings have been selected (Figure 4.4). The warning message of Figure 4.5 is then produced, and this warns that the restoration process must not be interrupted. Doing so is almost certain to leave the operating system with severe damage, and could possibly leave it in an unrepairable state. It also warns that the restoration is not reversible if this feature is being used with the computer in Safe Mode, or it is being run from an installation or rescue disc. Provided the System Restore process can be run from within Windows, it is normally possible to reverse the process or try a different restoration point.

Opting to go ahead with the restoration process results in a great deal of hard disc activity, a number of onscreen messages, and the computer eventually rebooting into Windows. Once into Windows there should be an onscreen message explaining that the restoration was completed successfully (Figure 4.6). With luck this will have cured the problem and the computer should operate normally.

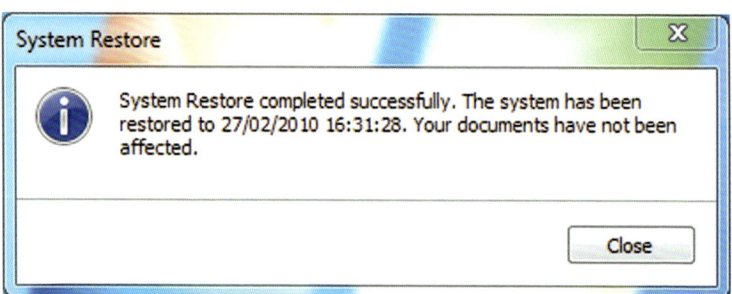

Fig.4.6 The restoration was completed successfully

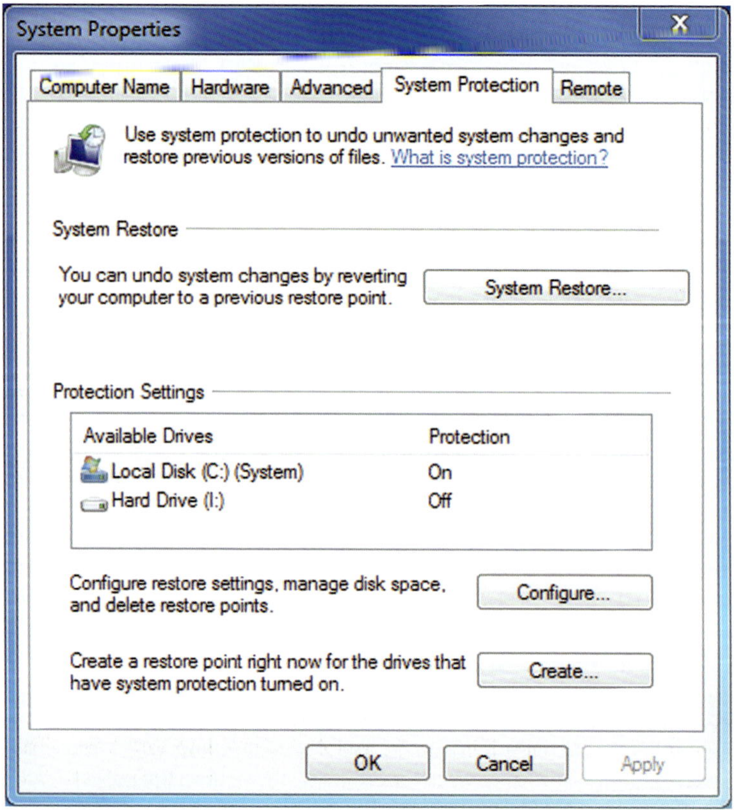

Fig.4.7 Select the System Protection tab

Making a point

Restoration points are produced automatically by Windows from time to time. For example, a restoration point is normally produced before any automatic update is installed, and when new application software is installed. This makes it easy to undo a problem that is introduced by an inappropriate update or a piece of "rogue" software. It also helps to ensure that there are plenty of restoration points to choose from if the program becomes unstable for any

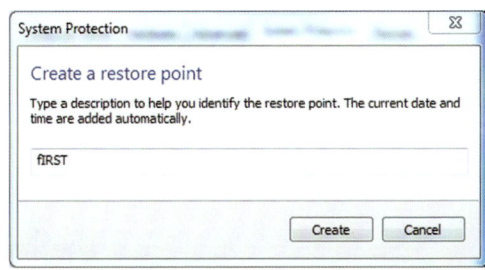

Fig.4.8 Enter a name for the restoration point

reason. As pointed out previously, they are also made by many tuning utilities prior to any changes being made to the operating system. It is not normally necessary, but if it is not done automatically at an appropriate juncture, a restoration point can be made manually at any time.

A restoration point is added by going to the System Properties window. This can be launched by going to the normal version of the Control Panel and operating the System and Security link. In the new version of the window operate the System link, and in the next version operate the "Advanced system settings" link. This launches the System Properties window, and it is the section under the System Protection tab (Figure 4.7) that is required. Operating the Create button near the bottom of the Window produces the small window of Figure 4.8, where a suitable name for the restoration point is added in the textbox. The time and date are automatically included by the operating system. Operating the Create button generates a new restoration point, and this will be confirmed by a small onscreen message.

Restore from boot disc

Provided the operating system is still largely intact, it is possible to use a restoration point even if it is not possible to boot into Windows. This feature can be accessed by booting into a Windows installation DVD or a system rescue disc. When booting from an installation disc, activate

Fig.4.9 Activate the "Repair your computer" link

the "Repair your computer" link when the screen of Figure 4.9 is reached. When booting from a rescue disc, opt to use the recovery tools when the window of Figure 4.10 is reached.

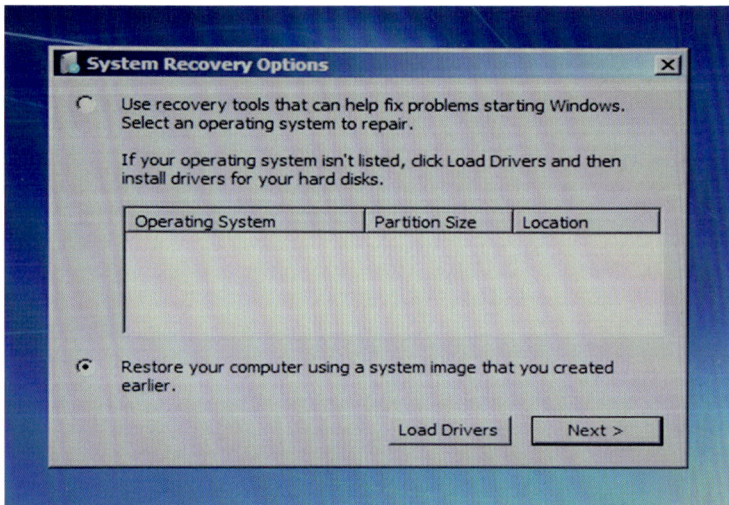

Fig.4.10 Opt to use the recovery tools when this screen is reached

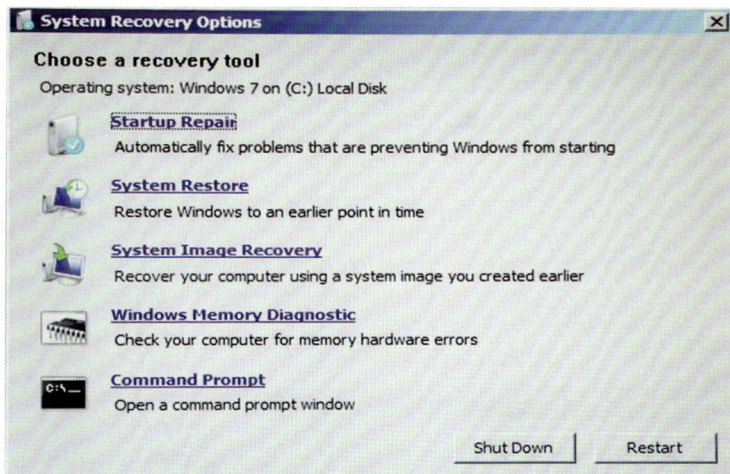

Fig.4.11 The System Recovery Options window

With either method the Recovery Tools window of Figure 4.11 should appear after a short delay while the appropriate files are loaded. From the list of options it is obviously System Restore that is selected, and this

Fig.4.12 The initial screen when entering the System Restore facility

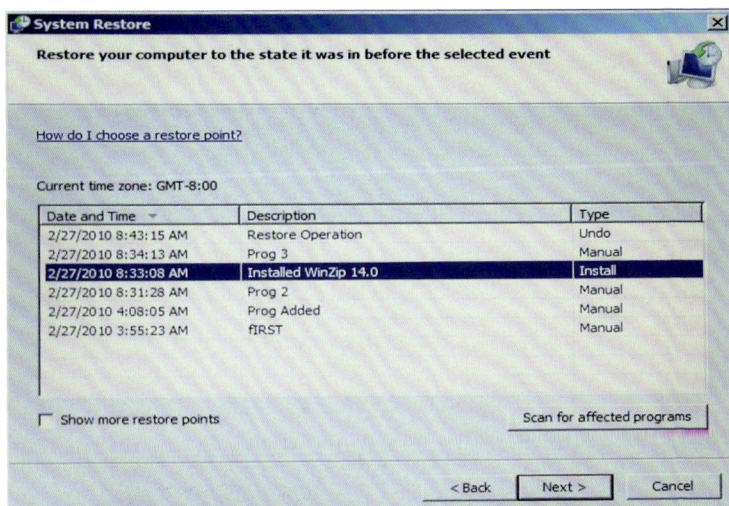

Fig.4.13 As before, the required restoration point can be selected

option produces the window of Figure 4.12. It is unlikely that a restoration point will be suggested here, and it is really just an information screen. Moving on to the next window (Figure 4.13), here you select the required restoration point. As before, it is possible to select a restoration point and then scan for affected programs and drivers.

Having selected a restoration point, operate the Next button to move on to the window (Figure 4.14). From here things operate from here much as they did before, with the selected restoration point being shown. Operating the Finish button brings up a warning message, and operating the Yes button starts the restoration process. Note that this process cannot be reversed when System Restore is run from a rescue or installation disc. The computer will eventually reboot into Windows, and (hopefully) the computer will then operate normally.

Defragmenters

Modern versions of Windows have some useful utilities as part of a standard installation, and it makes sense to utilise these rather than searching the Internet for free software that simply duplicates the built-in facilities of the operating system. Some PC tuning utilities seem to be little more than convenient front ends that make it easy to use the built-in

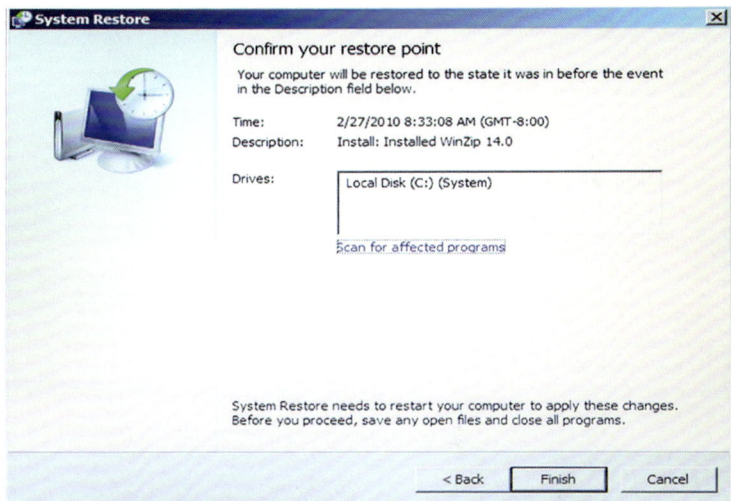

Fig.4.14 Operate the Finish button if the settings are correct

facilities of Windows. This is fine if you find it easier to use the utilities in this way, but some of the built-in utilities are fairly straightforward to use in their standard forms.

One of the most useful facilities is the often overlooked disc defragmenter. Many users tend to assume that files are automatically stored on the hard disc on the basis of one continuous section of disc per file. Unfortunately, it does not necessarily operate in this fashion. When Windows is first installed on a PC it is likely that files will be added in this fashion. The applications programs are then installed, and things will probably continue in an organised fashion with files stored on the disc as single clumps of data. Even if things have progressed well thus far, matters soon take a turn for the worse when the user starts deleting files, adding new files or programs, deleting more files, and so on.

Gaps are produced in the continuous block of data when files are deleted. Windows utilises the gaps when new data is added, but it will use them even if each one is not large enough to take a complete file. If necessary, it will use dozens of these small vacant areas to accommodate a large file. This can result in a large file being spread across the disc in numerous tiny packets of data, which makes reading the file a relatively slow and inefficient business. The computer can seriously slow down when a substantial number of files get fragmented in this way.

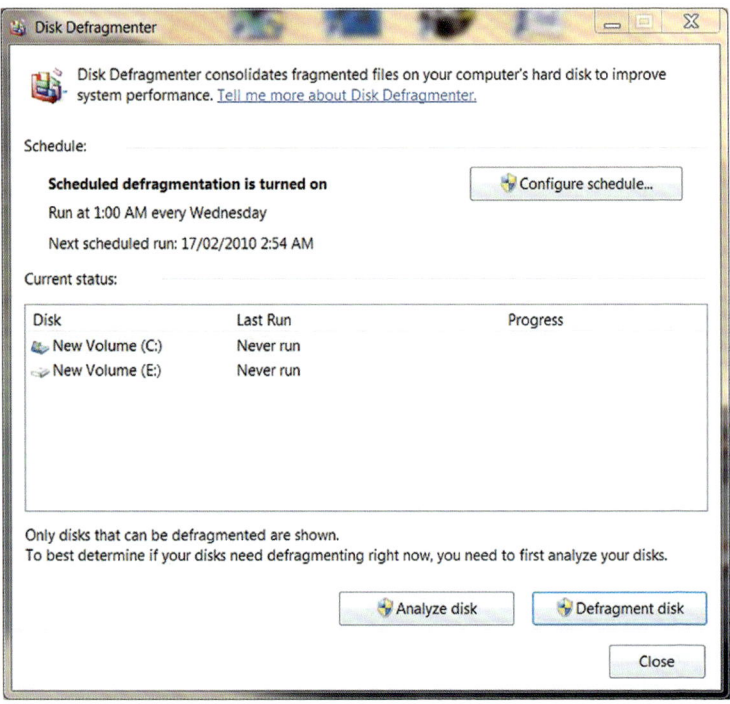

Fig.4.15 The initial screen of the defragmenter shows the drives that can be processed

The purpose of a disc defragmenter is to reorganise the files on a disc drive so that, as far as reasonably possible, large files are not fragmented. The built-in defragmenter of Windows 7 is available in the System Tools submenu as the Disk Defragmenter (Start – Accessories – System Tools – Disk Defragmenter). This utility has something of a chequered past, and in older versions of Windows it gave odd results with some disc drives. At some point in the proceedings the estimated time to completion would start to rise and usually kept rising with the process never finishing! Provided you are using a reasonably modern version of Windows there should be no problem of this type and the Disk Defragmenter program should work well. There should certainly be no problem with the Windows XP/Vista/7 versions.

On launching the defragmenter program a window like the one shown in Figure 4.15 is produced. The main panel lists the disc drives that can be processed by the program, and in this case the computer's two hard

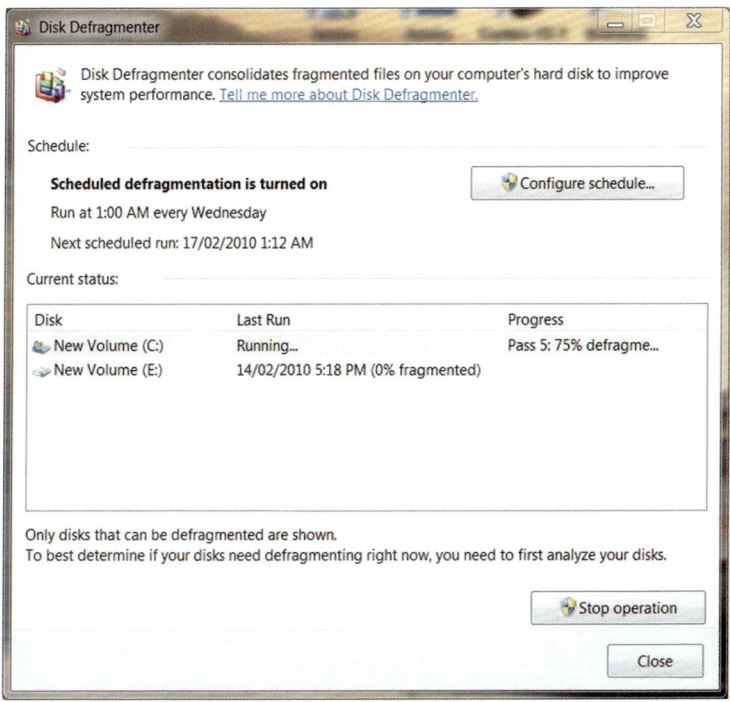

Fig.4.16 The program shows how things are progressing

disc drives are listed. These are physically two separate hard disc drives, but it is actually the logical disc drives that the program lists. In other words, if the computer has (say) one hard disc drive with three partitions, each partition will be listed separately. The partitions are treated as three separate entities by the operating system, and they are therefore processed in that way by defragmenter programs.

While it is possible to jump straight in and start processing the selected drive, this version of Disk Defragmenter offers the alternative of first analysing the drive to determine how badly (or otherwise) it is fragmented. There is little point in wasting time defragmenting a disc that is performing well. To analyse the disc operate the Analyze Disk button near the bottom of the window. The test result is in the form of a percentage, and Microsoft recommends defragmenting the disc if the result is ten percent or more.

In this case drive C: did require defragmentation, but with a result of zero percent for drive D:, it was only drive C: that needed processing. Drive

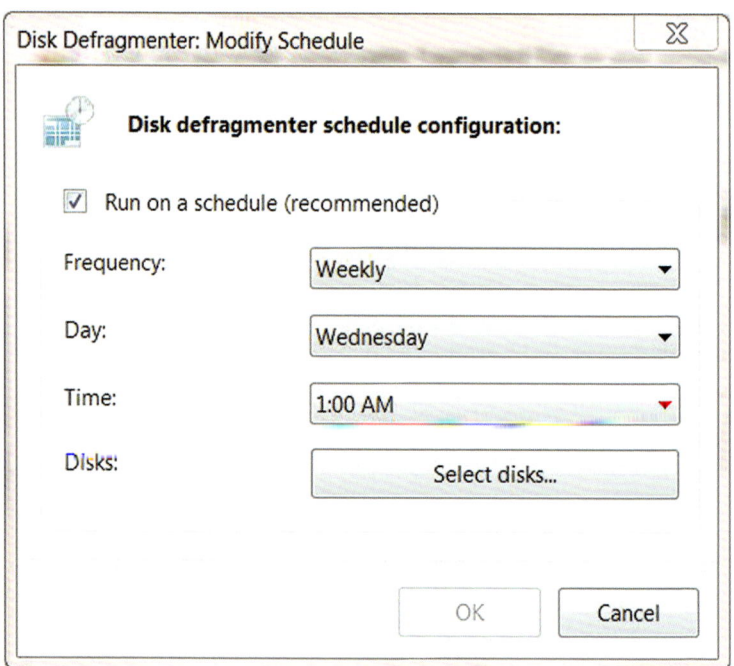

Fig.4.17 The defragmenter can be scheduled to run automatically

C: was therefore selected and the Defragment Disk button was operated. The program keeps you informed of what it is doing Figure 4.16, but unlike most previous versions it does not give an estimate of the remaining time required to complete the task. It is not usually quick though, and can take an hour or more with a large disc that is badly fragmented. It is never possible to fully defragment the disc, and it is not really necessary to do so. The program should defragment the disc enough to give a significant improvement in performance, and to get the drive operating at something close to its optimum level.

Regular use of Disk Defragmenter should get the disc to the point where it is fully defragmented, or nearly so, and should maintain it close to optimum performance. The defragmenter program can be set to run automatically, and the idea is to schedule it to run at a time when the computer will usually be operating, but will be receiving little or no use. In order to schedule automatic operation it is merely necessary to operate the Configure Schedule button, and then use the dialogue box (Figure

4.17) to select the required time and frequency, and the disc or discs to be processed.

Tuning utilities

There are numerous utility programs for use with Windows, offering facilities such as Widows Registry scanning and cleaning, disc defragmentation, and the removal of unnecessary files from the hard disc drive. There are numerous free and commercial programs of this type, and some of the free programs offer a good range of facilities and perform well. Before buying any software of this type it is certainly worth trying one or two of the better free programs to see if they fulfil your requirements.

You have to be especially careful when this type of software since it can seriously damage the operating system if it is not written properly. Also, bogus utility software has long been a popular way of attacking computers and infecting them with viruses, Trojans, spyware, and other malicious software. Another point to bear in mind is software of this type can do more harm than good unless it is written specifically for the particular version of Windows in use. Before downloading and installing any software of this type you need to ensure that it is of reasonable quality, and download sites that include software reviews can be very helpful here. It is also best to download it from a reliable source, and check carefully that it is recommended for use with the version of Windows installed on your PC.

Registry problem?

An error or series of errors in the Windows Registry is a common source of Windows problems. Registry errors are behind many Windows problems where the system behaves in an odd or erratic fashion. Errors in the Registry can also cause start-up and shutdown problems, a slowing of the system, programs "freezing", and so on.

The Windows Registry is a database that contains various operating parameters for Windows itself, and for any substantial piece of application software. When you change things like the screen resolution, the background for the Windows Desktop, or practically any aspect of Windows, you are actually changing one or more entries in the Registry. Those who know what they are doing can alter parameters by directly editing the Registry rather than by using the built-in facilities of Windows. Directly tweaking the Registry used to be a common practice among

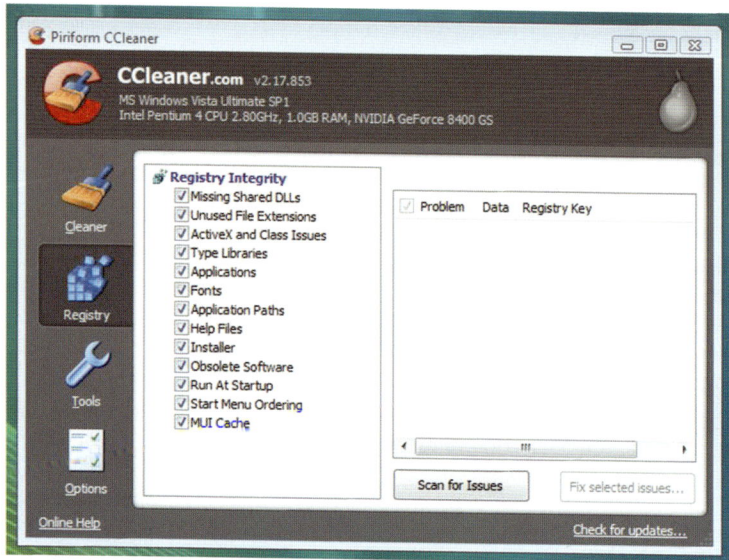

Fig.4.18 The Registry section of the CCleaner program

Windows experts as it permitted some changes that could not be achieved by other means. It now seems to be far less popular than in the past. **Anyway, it is certainly something that should not be attempted by those who lack the necessary expertise.** When directly altering the Registry it is easy to get it slightly wrong and make matters worse instead of curing the problem.

The normal approach to curing Windows Registry problems is to use a utility program that searches the Registry for errors, and fixes any that it finds. No program of this type can be guaranteed to work perfectly every time, and the program should enable a backup copy of the Registry to be made before it undertakes the scanning and correction process. It is then possible to revert to the backup copy if the Registry fixing program should happen to make things worse rather than better. However, it is definitely better not to get into this situation in the first place, and it is important to use a Registry checker that is tried, tested and as reliable as it could reasonably be.

The program used in this example is CCleaner, which is free, but you can make a donation to the author if you find the program useful. Any search engine should soon come up with a few sites that offer this program as a free download. CCleaner is a popular utility program that

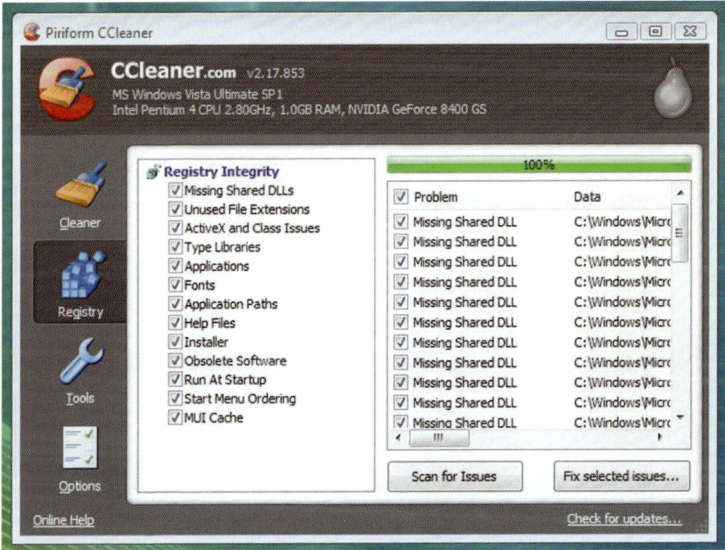

Fig.4.19 There will often be a long list of detected problems

has a good track record, and represents a safe option provided it is obtained from a reputable download site. CCleaner is actually rather more than a Registry checker, and it offers other features such as one that offers similar facilities to the Windows Disk Cleanup facility. For the moment we will only consider its use as a Registry checker and fixer.

Once running, and with the Registry button selected in the right-hand section of the window, CCleaner provides a list of things that can be checked (Figure 4.18). All the checkboxes will be ticked by default so that all the tests are carried out, and it is probably best to leave things this way. Operate the Scan for Issues button to start the checking process, which will probably take a minute or three. If any problems are found, and they usually are, a scrollable list will be produced in the right-hand panel of the window (Figure 4.19).

A brief description of each problem is given, and there is a checkbox for each entry. All the checkboxes are ticked by default, but you can remove the tick is there is a problem that you would prefer the program to leave untouched. Operate the Fix Selected Issues button when you are ready for the program to go ahead and make the changes to the Registry. You may be asked to confirm some changes (Figure 4.20), and it is just a

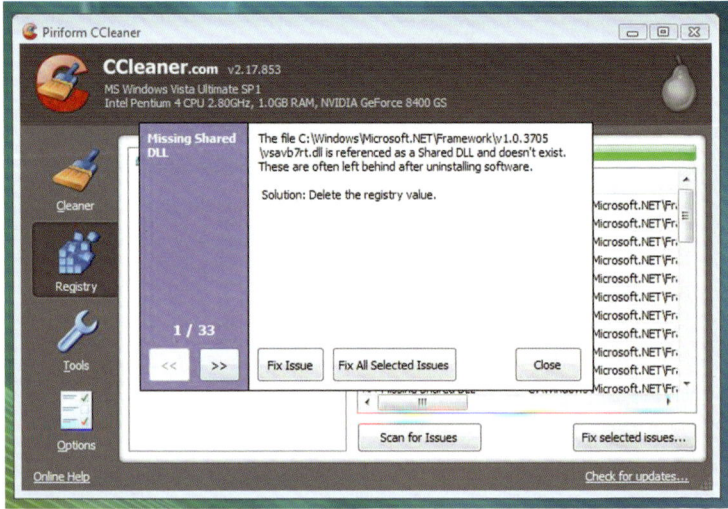

Fig.4.20 You will be asked to confirm that some changes should be made

matter of operating the Fix Issue button to confirm that you would like the change to be made. Operate the Fix All Selected Issues button if you would prefer to have the program proceed without asking your permission again.

Of course, any program of this type has its limitations. If it finds reference to a nonexistent DLL file in the Registry it cannot reinstate the missing file, so it takes the alternative course of deleting the reference to it. The missing file is probably not needed any longer, and its reference in the Registry is probably something that an uninstaller has failed to deal with properly. If the file is still needed and its absence results in an application program failing to work properly, reinstalling the application should reinstate the file and cure the problem.

As pointed out previously, CCleaner can do more than Registry checking. Amongst other things, it can check the hard disc drives for unnecessary files (Figure 4.21), and erase the selected files to free hard disc space. In this example it found about 435 megabytes of temporary files, etc., that were not needed. Apart from wasting hard disc space, large numbers of temporary and other unnecessary files can tend to slow down the system.

There is a similar, if slightly less sophisticated disc cleaning utility built into Windows. It can be launched by going to the Start menu and

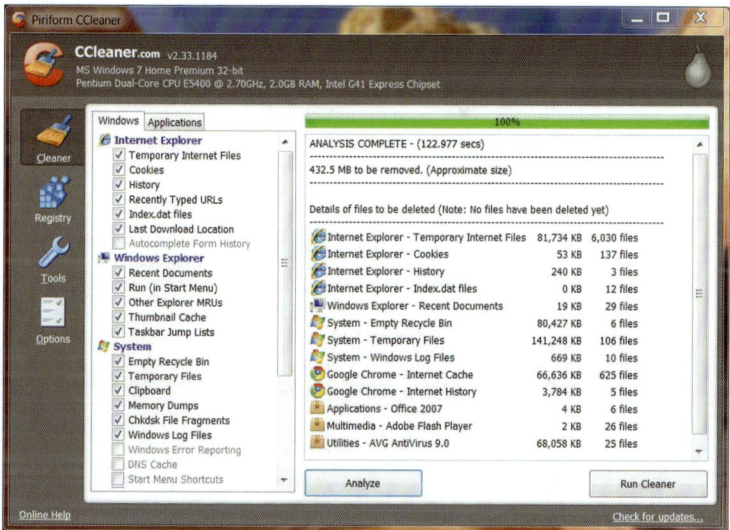

Fig.4.21 CCleaner can check discs for unnecessary files

selecting All Programs – Accessories – System Tools – Disk Cleanup. Initially there is a small window (Figure 4.22) where the disc to be cleaned is selected. If you need to clean more than one disc they must be dealt with separately. Having selected the required drive from the drop-down menu, left-clicking the OK button starts the scan, and after a short delay the results will be displayed (Figure 4.23). The middle part of the window provides a description of a selected file type. It is then a matter of going down the list and making sure that the appropriate check boxes are ticked. With anything like this it is best to err on the side of caution, and

files should be left intact if you are not sure whether they are still needed.

More options are available if you operate the Cleanup System Files button, and then choose the appropriate hard disc drive again when the small menu window

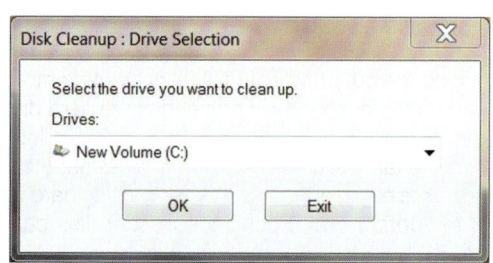

Fig.4.22 Select the required disc from the drop-down menu

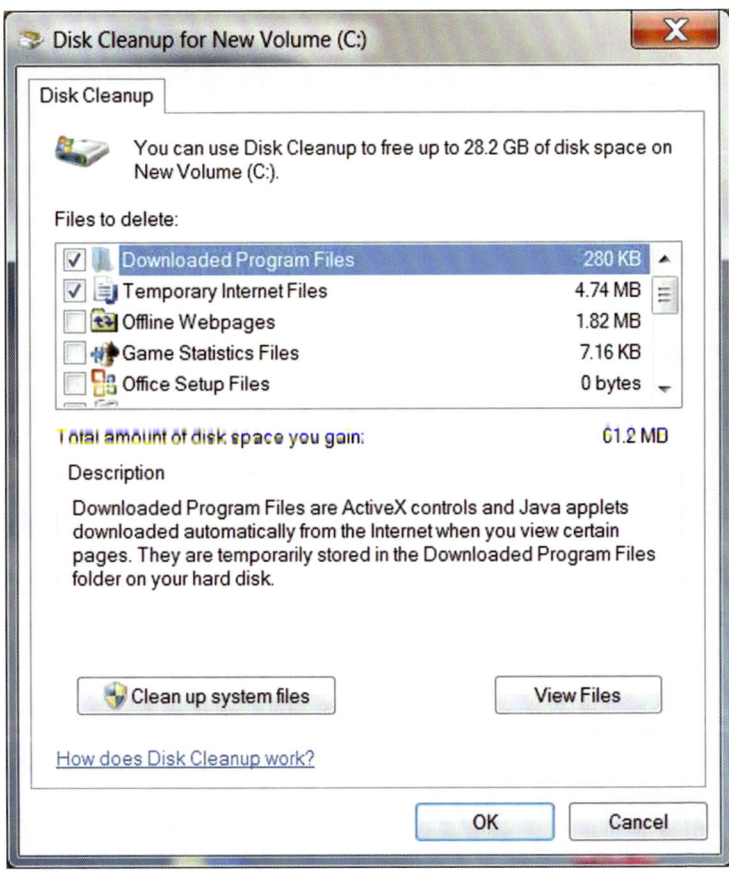

Fig.4.23 You can select the types of file that will be erased

appears again. In the new version of the Disk Cleanup window (Figure 4.24) there is a More Options tab, and the window changes to the one of Figure 4.25 when this is selected. The Clean up button in the upper part of the window simply launches the Windows Uninstaller utility, and hard disc space can then be freed by removing any programs that are no longer used. The Clean-up button in the lower part of the window is used if you wish to remove restoration points other than the most recent one, which can sometimes free a large amount of hard disc space. It can also remove any old backup files produced by the Windows Backup

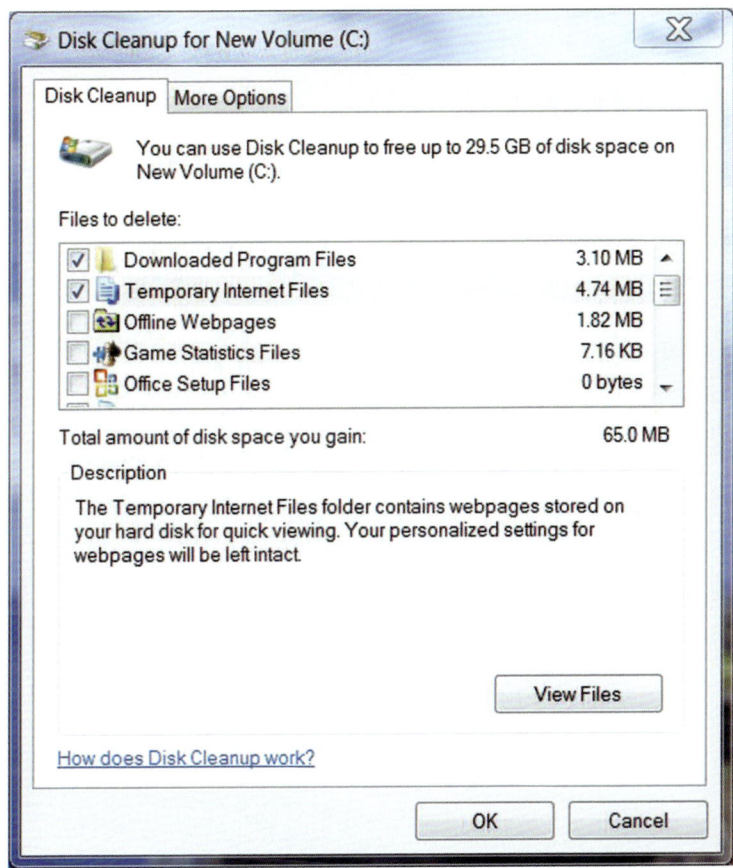

Fig.4.24 Select the More Options tab

utility, which can again free a substantial amount of hard disc space. In either case it should only be used if the system has been operating in a trouble-free fashion for some time, and there is little likelihood of older restoration points or backups being required.

Background processes

The Tools section of CCleaner provides access to the Windows Uninstaller and System Restore facilities, and to a utility that provides some control

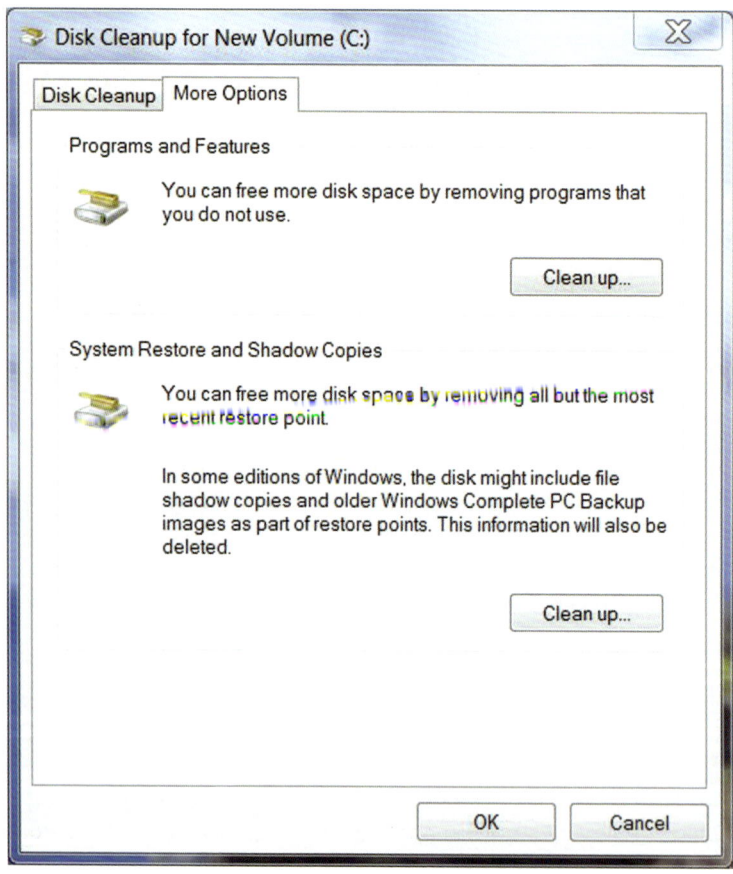

Fig.4.25 Old System Restore points can be deleted here

over the programs that are launched automatically at start-up (Figure 4.26). It is not normal application programs that we are concerned with here, but what are termed "background processes", or just "processes". Background processes are important to modern computing and provide a number of useful tasks. For example, an antivirus program running in the background can protect your PC from infection, dealing with viruses and computer pests before they have a chance to do any harm.

The problem with background processes is that too many of them running at the same time can hog a PC's resources. The processing time and

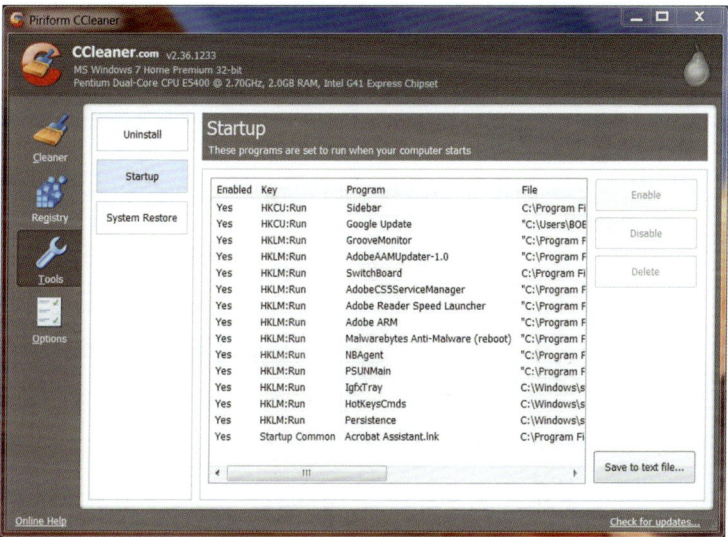

Fig.4.26 Unnecessary background processes can be switched off

memory used by each process will probably be quite small, but with ten processes running the overall drain on the PC's resources could be considerable. In fact having a large number of these processes running simultaneously would almost certainly slow down even the most potent of PCs.

A big problem with background processes is that many of them are installed automatically when applications programs are loaded onto a PC. The installation program might explain that a background process will be installed, and there is sometimes an option to omit it from the installation. In practice few users pay any attention to these options when installing new software. If you simply opt for "default" or "typical" installations it is likely that your PC will soon be running some additional background tasks. With some installers you are simply not given any choice, and the background tasks are always installed, although the application program might include a means of switching them off.

The exact purpose of some background processes is less than obvious, but many of them are intended to make things happen faster when using a certain facility of an application program. This is fine if you make frequent use of the program and facility in question, but the overhead on the PC's

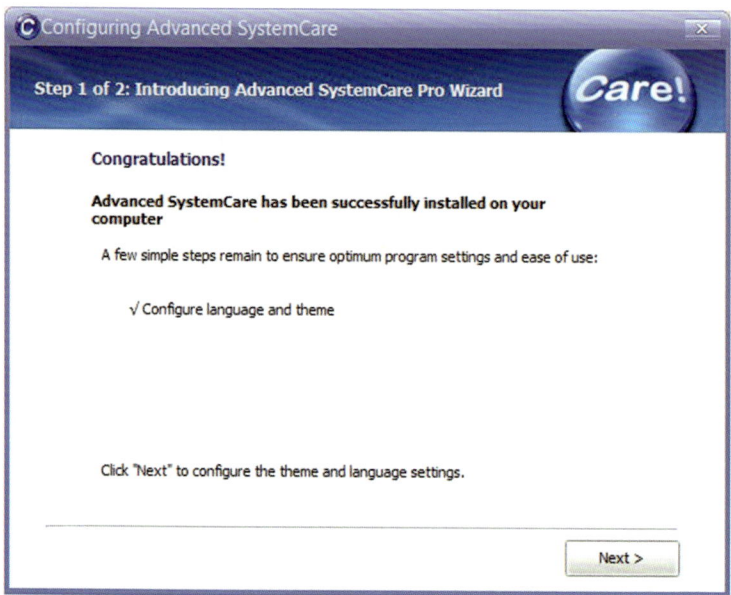

Fig.4.27 The initial screen is an information type

performance is unlikely to be justified in the case of an infrequently used feature. Where possible, it makes sense to suppress background tasks that do not "earn their keep".

Using CCleaner it is possible to go through the background tasks, selecting and disabling any that are deemed unnecessary. If you find that disabling a process results in the loss of an important function, it is easy to reinstate it. Just go back to the relevant section of CCleaner, select the process, and operate the Enable button. Note that any changes to the start-up processes will not normally be implemented until the computer has been rebooted.

Advanced SystemCare

Probably the most popular free tuning program at present is the free version of Advanced System   Care. This is available from the usual sources of free software, such as CNET.com. The information window of Figure 4.27 appears the first time the program is run, and at the next

Fig.4.28 The required theme and language are selected here

screen (Figure 4.28) the radio buttons and drop-down menus are used to select the required theme and language respectively. Moving on, the small window of Figure 4.29 gives an opportunity to create a restoration point before running and using the program, and it is advisable to do so.

The main program is then launched (Figure 4.30). Operating the top button in the left-hand section of the window takes the program into the Maintain Windows section (Figure 4.31). This offers facilities such as Registry and disc cleaners. Operating the Settings tab launches a new window (Figure 4.32) that gives tremendous control over the tasks the program will perform,

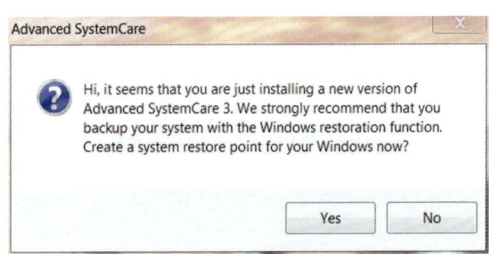

Fig.4.29 It is advisable to take the opportunity of adding a restoration point

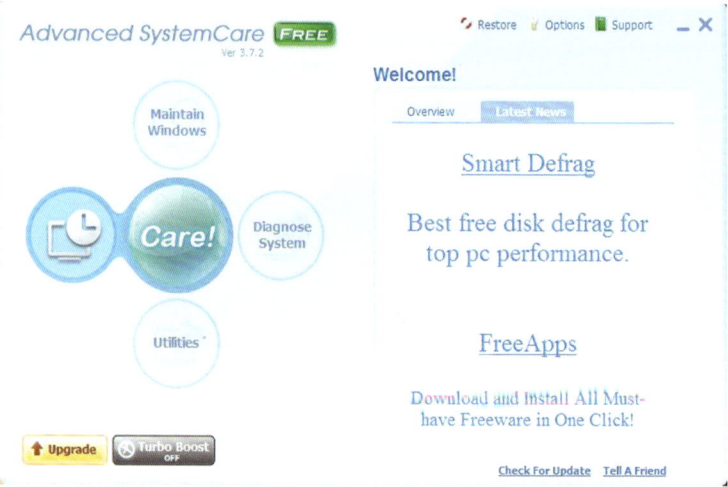

Fig.4.30 The initial screen of the main program

but the default settings will usually suffice. For this example I ran the Spyware Removal and Junk Files Clean utilities, and obtained the result shown in Figure 4.33. Left-clicking the red link text produces more details

Fig.4.31 The Maintain Windows section of the program

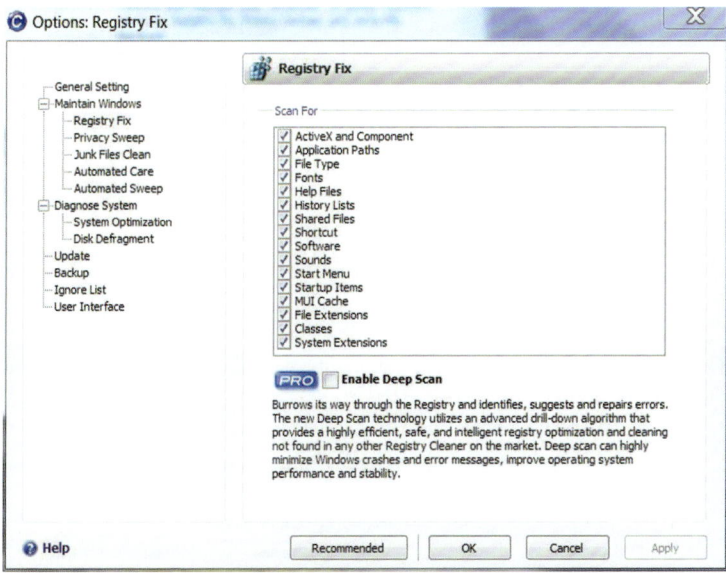

Fig.4.32 You are provided with plenty of control over the tasks the
program will perform

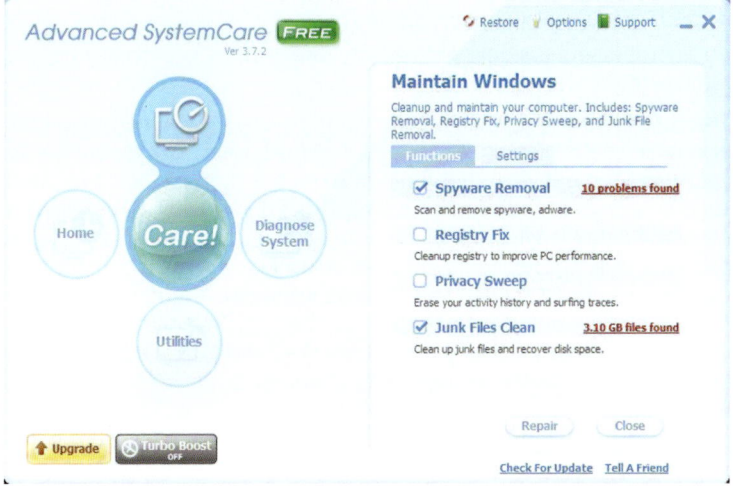

Fig.4.33 The results obtained from running two of the tools

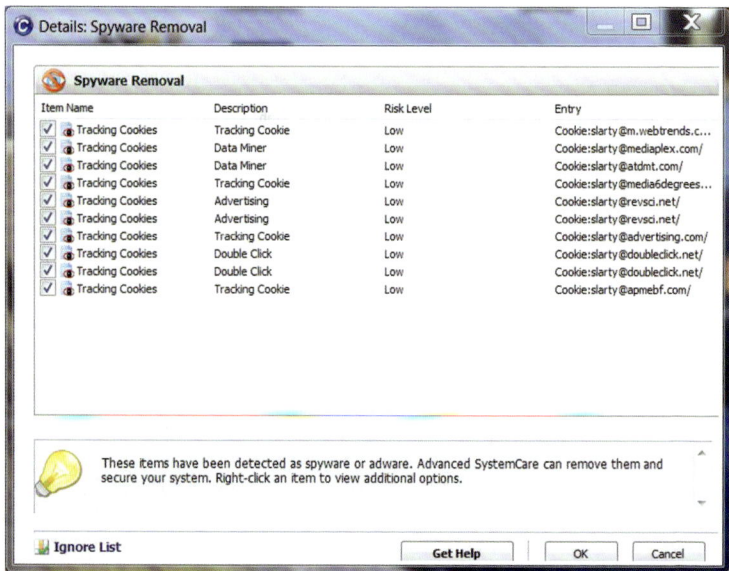

Fig.4.34 The detailed report from the Spyware Removal facility

of that set of results, and Figure 4.34 shows the detailed results for the Spyware Removal tool. The items found are all tracking cookies, which do not represent a significant security threat, but it is probably best to remove them.

The results from the junk file removal utility are shown in Figure 4.35, and most of the files are temporary Windows files. The amount is so vast (over 3 gigabytes) that most of them are probably left over from various upgrades, updates, and backups. It is unlikely that a disc cleaning utility will delete anything vital, but with anything like this it is best to be cautious, with files not being removed unless you are reasonably certain that they will not be needed again. Deleting things like temporary Internet files is risk free, but with something like the recycle bin it is perhaps as well to check that the files are definitely not needed any more. Having used the checkboxes to make any changes to the files that will be removed, operate the Repair button back in the main window to actually remove the selected files. If there are a large number of files this could take a while, and the program will indicate its progress via the usual bargraph (Figure 4.36).

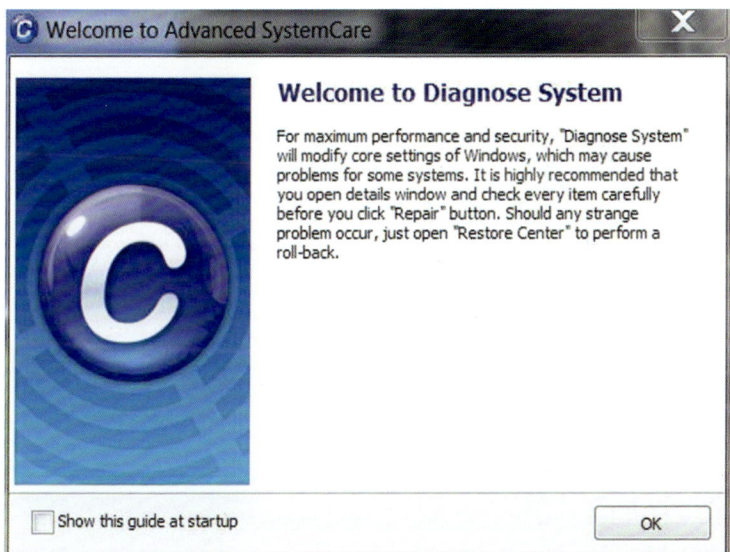

Fig.4.39 This warning appears when using the Diagnose System facility

I ran the Registry Fix tool separately, and it found a large number of problems (Figure 4.37). As before, more details of the scan results (Figure 4.38) can be obtained by left-clicking the red link text, but these may not be particularly helpful unless you are reasonable expert at the internal working of Windows. For most users it is just a matter of accepting the scan results at face value and letting the program do its stuff.

Privacy Sweep

Amongst other things, the Privacy Sweep tool removes traces of your Internet surfing so that no one can use your computer to find the Internet sites and pages that you have visited. This type of thing is fine if you value your privacy, and you do not want others prying into your Internet activities. However, you need to be aware that there is a downside, which is that deleting the Internet history files could make it difficult for you to retrace your steps and find a site that you visited earlier in the day, or perhaps a week ago. If you are going to use any privacy facility of this type it is important make a note of any Internet addresses that you might wish to revisit, and they should obviously be stored where others do not have easy access to them.

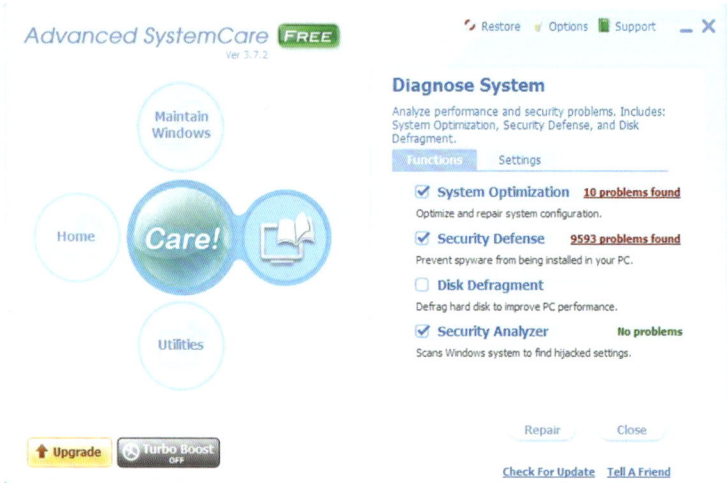

Fig.4.40 There are four facilities in the Diagnose System section

Diagnose System

Operating the Diagnose System button produces the warning message of Figure 4.39. This recommends that changes should only be made using this section of the program after they have been reviewed, and the user is sure that the changes are safe. It also explains that the changes can be reversed using the Restore Center.   Once into the Diagnose System utility, there are again four facilities listed in the right-hand section of the window (Figure 4.40). The first of these is used to optimise the system and repair any damage that is found. The second section is the Security Defense utility, which tries to protect the system from spyware. The third is a disc defragmenter, and the last one checks the system for any settings that have been hijacked by malicious software.

I used the first, second, and fourth sections, and as can be seen from Figure 4.40, problems were found by the Security Optimisation and Security Defense sections. As before, left-clicking the red link text produces more details of the problems (Figures 4.41 and 4.42). After reviewing the results and deselecting any that are deemed unnecessary, operating the Repair button back in the main window actually implements the changes.

Using the Disc Defragmenter tool results in the disc being scanned and a report being produced. Once again, operating the red link text displays

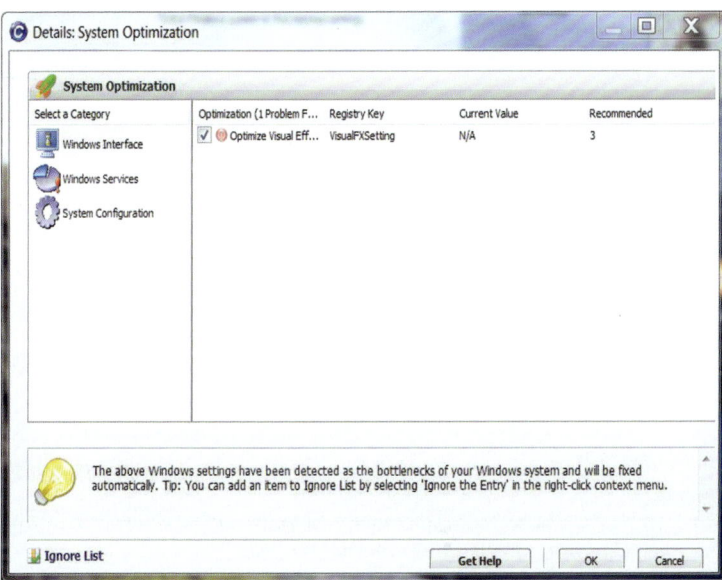

Fig.4.41 More details of the detected System Optimisation problems are available

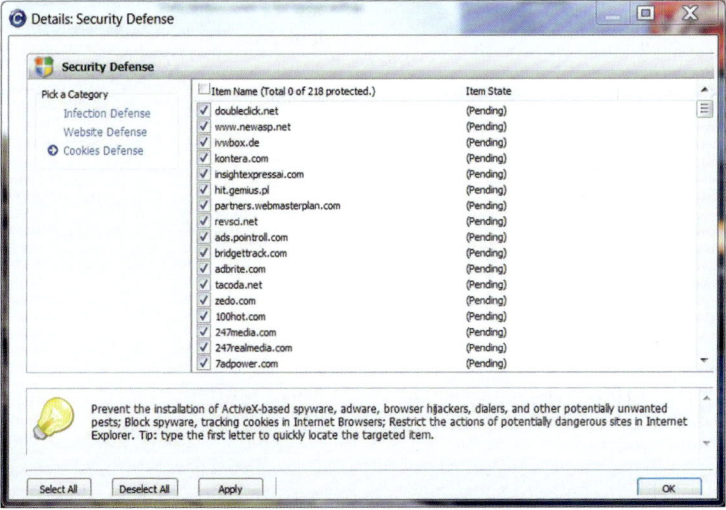

Fig.4.42 The detailed version of the Security Defense results

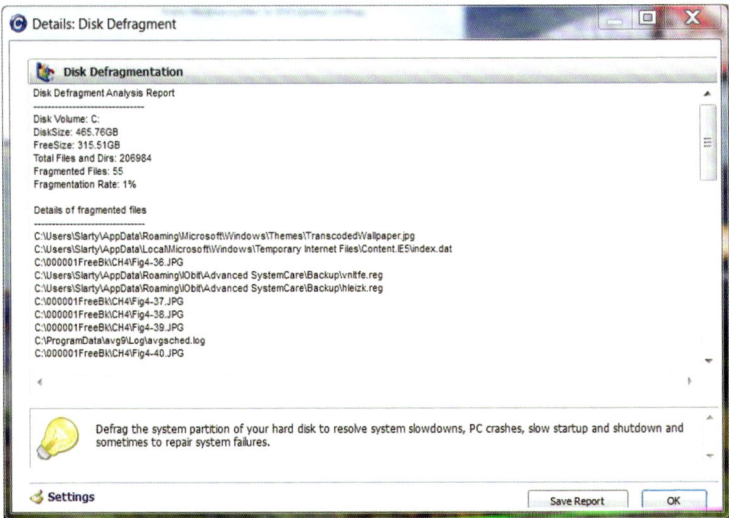

Fig.4.43 The report from the Defragmenter utility

the results (Figure 4.43), and using the Repair button in the main window actually sets the defragmenter into action. In this case the degree of fragmentation was quite low at only one percent. It is not usually deemed worthwhile defragmenting a disc unless the amount of fragmentation is at least a few percent. In fact many consider that the threshold is about ten percent, and that there is no point in using a defragmenter unless the degree of fragmentation is above this figure. On the other hand, defragmenting the disc will not do any harm, and with a small amount of fragmentation it should not take long to complete the task. Waiting until there is a large amount of fragmentation can make the defragmentation a long and slow process, especially if the hard disc drive is nearly full. It is better to use periodic defragmentation to prevent a high degree of fragmentation building up.

Disk Doctor

The lower button in the main window provides access to various utilities (Figure 4.44), one of which is the Disk Doctor. It is still at the beta test stage in the latest version of the program available at the time of writing this, which makes it difficult to recommend, although it worked well enough when I tried it. The first task when using this utility is to select

Fig.4.44 Various additional tune-up utilities are available

the drive or drives that will be checked Figure 4.45. For this example drive C was selected. The program will then analyse the disc (Figure 4.46), which will probably take a few minutes. Having completed the

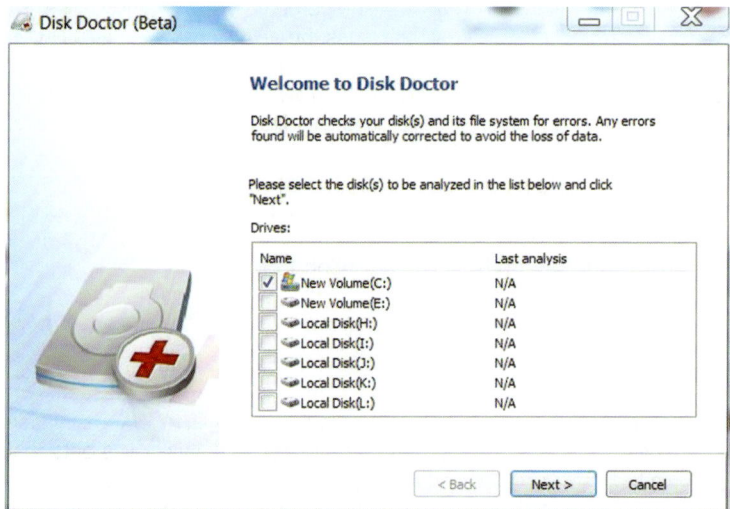

Fig.4.45 Disk Doctor will check the selected drives

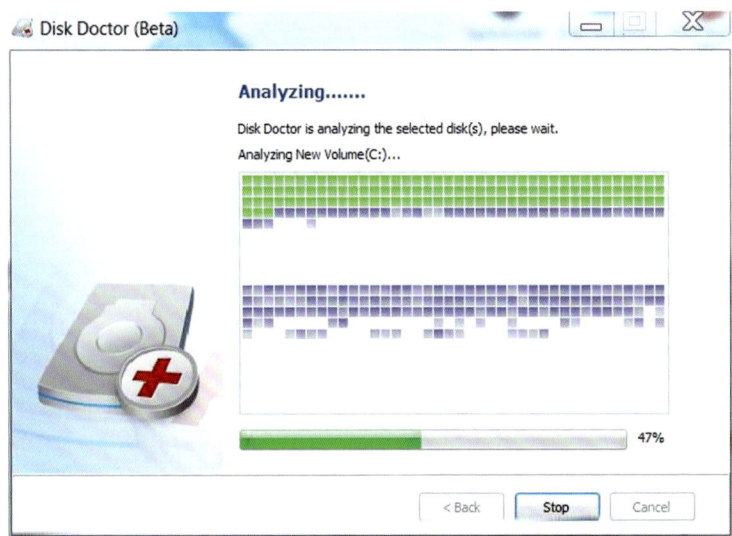

Fig.4.46 The disc checking process is in progress

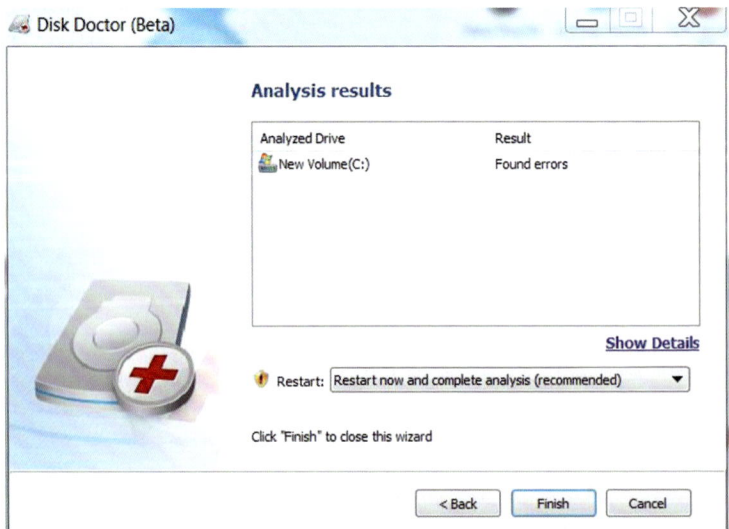

Fig.4.47 In this example some disc errors have been found

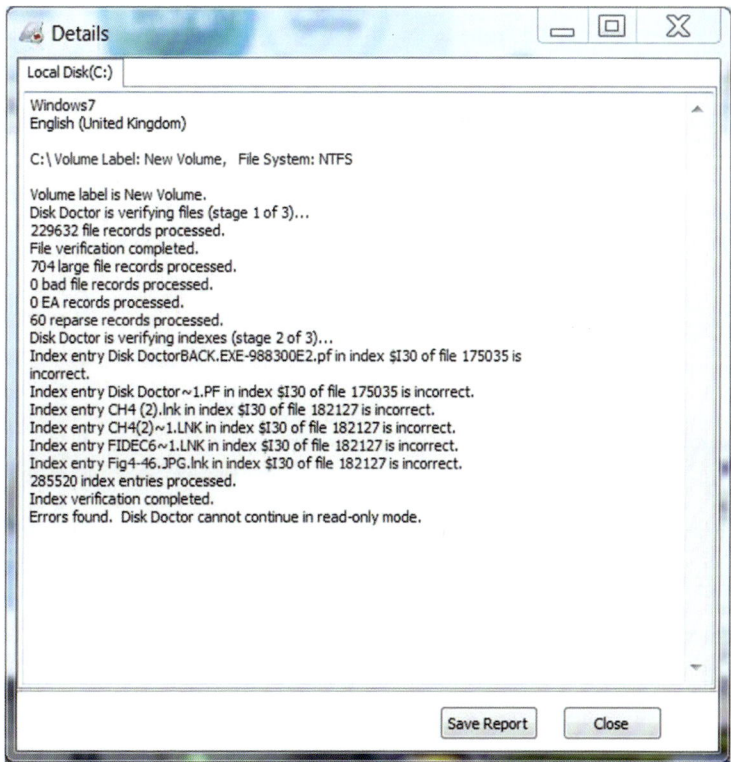

Fig.4.48 The program can show details of the errors found

analysis it will then indicate whether any errors have been found (Figure 4.47). Operating the Show Details link produces a list of any errors found (Figure 4.48). The computer must be restarted in order to complete the process, and it is quite normal for disc checking and repair programs to require a reboot at some point in the proceedings. This is usually so that the process can be completed before the computer boots into Windows, and restrictions are placed on the ways in which the drive can be handled.

Built-in disc checking

Using any disc checking and repair utility runs a certain amount of risk, and any important files must be backed up onto another physical drive before using one. There is a disc checking facility built into Windows 7,

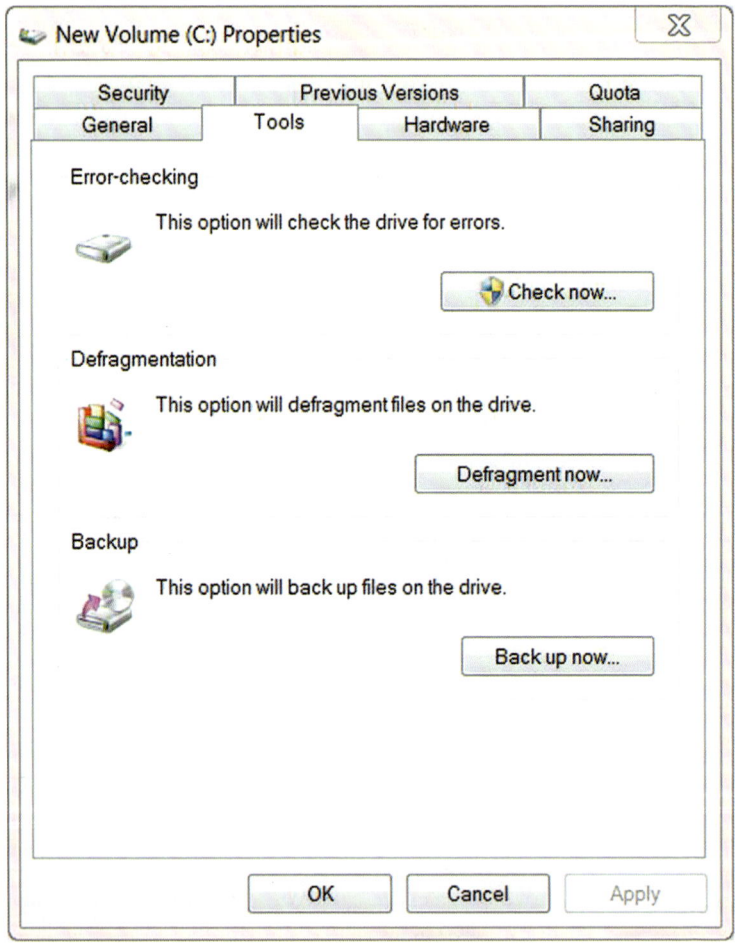

Fig.4.49 The Tools section includes a disc checking facility

and this probably represents the safest option, and it is probably best to try the built-in facility before looking for other solutions. Using the built-in facility it is usually possible for this to repair problems with the disc filing system so that the computer can operate normally thereafter.

However, this is not to say that it will be possible to recover any data that was damaged as a result of problems with the filing system. While it might be possible to recover some fragments of data, the chances of them being of any practical use are very slim. The same thing is true when using any disc checking and repair software. Data that has been overwritten cannot be recovered. Of course, a disc checking facility cannot make repairs if the problem is in the hardware. It can only

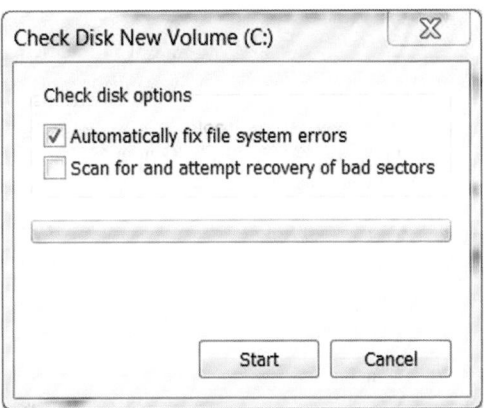

Fig.4.50 Two types of checking are available

confirm that there is a hardware fault. It is possible to have the system ignore bad sectors of the disc that are found, but when a disc drive starts to become unreliable it is definitely a good idea to replace it rather than avoiding the bad bits and hoping for the best.

The Windows disc checking program is easily accessed, and the first step is to go into Windows Explorer. Locate the entry for the drive you wish to check, right-click its entry, and then choose Properties from the pop-up menu. This produces a window that gives some basic information about the drive.

Operate the Tools tab to switch to a Window like the one in Figure 4.49, which includes an error checking facility. Left-clicking the Check Now button produces the small window of Figure 4.50, where two options are available via the checkboxes. The upper checkbox is ticked if you wish to check the filing system, but this check cannot be made while Windows is running. Using this option schedules the check to run the next time the computer is booted into Windows. Using the facilities offered by the lower checkbox is more straightforward. This checks the disc for bad sectors, and using this option results in the disc being checked immediately.

If you opt to have the file system checked, on starting the scan you will instead get a pop-up message that explains the need to provide the scan just before the computer boots into Windows. Opt to go ahead anyway, and then you are then asked if you would like to schedule the scan to be run automatically on the next occasion that the computer is

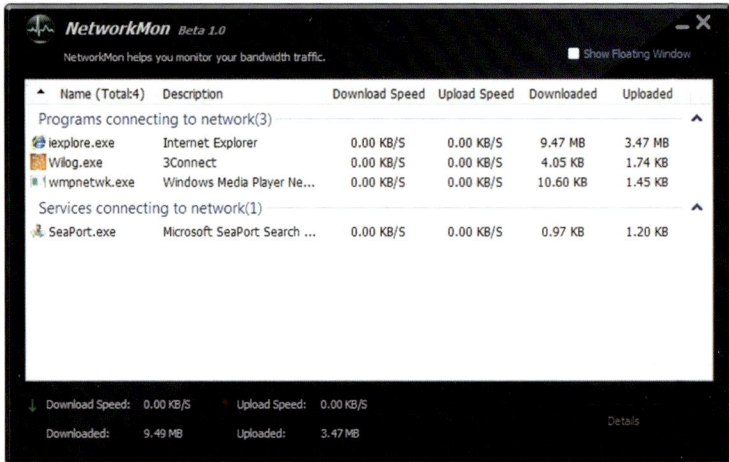

Fig.4.51   The program includes a useful network monitor

booted into Windows. To go ahead with the checking and fixing process, operate the Yes button and restart the computer. The checking program will be launched during the boot process before the boot drive is left with any open files. The screen will show how things are progressing, and the boot process will continue once the disc checker has completed its task.

Network and memory

There are a couple of useful utilities in the additional tools section of Advanced SystemCare, and one of these is a network monitor (Figure 4.51). I recently had problems with the rate at which the monthly allowance for my mobile broadband connection was being used. It was clearly reducing far faster than normal, but the built-in monitor of Windows was of limited help. It enabled me to see when the amount of data being downloaded was excessive, but it did not show which program was responsible for the problem. The network monitor of Advanced SystemCare is much more help in this respect, as it provides individual statistics for each program and service that is connected to the network.

The other tool worthy of investigation is the Smart RAM memory utility. This enables memory usage to be monitored (Figure 4.52), and it also has facilities for freeing memory that has become unnecessarily tied up by the operating system. Windows XP is notorious for reserving large

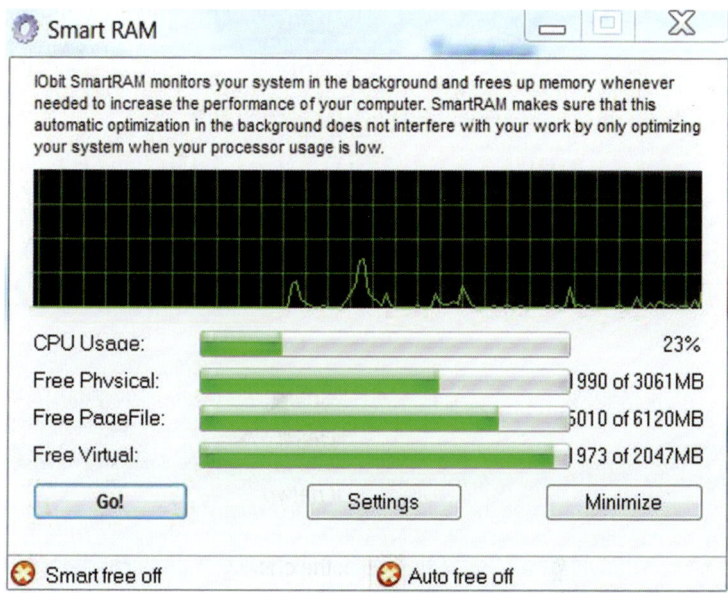

Fig.4.52 *Memory usage can be monitored and improved*

amounts of memory, presumably to cache files, leaving too little free for application programs to run properly. Windows Vista and 7 seem to be less prone to this problem, but you can still find that a task such as copying large amounts of data from one drive to another tends to leave application programs running at a snail's pace for some time thereafter. A program such as Smart RAM can remove the unnecessary hogging of memory resources and get the computer back to its normal operating conditions and speed.

Action Center

Windows XP has a troubleshooting wizard that can be used to help solve a wide variety of problems. Unfortunately, there is no equivalent feature in Windows Vista, and no exact equivalent in Windows 7 either. However, there is a troubleshooting facility available via the Action Center, and this covers a useful range of problems. The Action Center can be accessed by going to the Control Panel, selecting one of the icon views, and double-clicking the Action Center icon. Once into the Action Center, activate the Troubleshooting link.

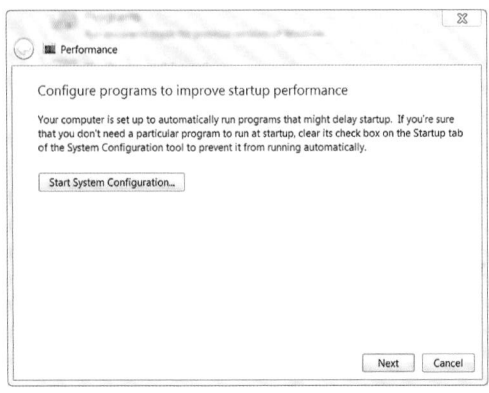

Fig.4.53 The program has a recommendation

The two buttons near the top of the window are used to opt for the latest troubleshooting content or use only the standard content. It is best to opt for the latest content if the computer has an active Internet connection. There are links to various types of troubleshooting help such as audio devices and other hardware, security, programs, performance issues and Internet connection problems. Sometimes the help is in standard wizard form, while in other cases it is largely automatic. If your computer has a problem in one of the areas covered by this troubleshooting facility, it might provide the quickest and easiest way of sorting things out.

Of most interest in the current context, is that there is a troubleshooter for dealing with performance issues. It is launched by choosing the "Check for performance issues" option, and it produces a window that is really just an information box that briefly explains the purpose of this troubleshooter. This is to check for problems that will not bring the computer to a complete standstill, but might reduce its performance in some way. Operating the Advanced link produces a checkbox, and problems will be automatically repaired if this checkbox is ticked. Operating the Next button starts the checking, and after a few seconds the program will either report that it has completed its task, or it will suggest a course of action by the user.

In this example it detected a large number of programs being run automatically at start-up, and it recommended disabling any of these programs that were unnecessary (Figure 4.53). As pointed out previously, unless you know what you are doing it is best not to dabble with this type of thing. However, if you are sufficiently expert to select the unnecessary programs it is worth trying this feature. Operating the Start System Configuration button launches the System Configuration window at the appropriate section. Here it is just a matter of unticking the checkbox for any program that you do not wish to run when the operating system starts up.

Index